SURVEY

SOUL-BODY INTERACTION

The Portable New Century Edition of

EMANUEL SWEDENBORG'S

SURVEY

Translated from the Latin by Jonathan S. Rose

and

SOUL-BODY INTERACTION

Translated from the Latin by George F. Dole

SWEDENBORG FOUNDATION

West Chester, Pennsylvania

Originally published in Latin as two separate works:

>Survey: *Summaria Expositio Doctrinae Novae Ecclesiae, Quae per Novam Hierosolymam in Apocalypsi Intelligitur* (Amsterdam, 1769)
>Soul-Body Interaction: *De Commercio Animae et Corporis, Quod Creditur Fieri vel per Influxum Physicum, vel per Influxum Spiritualem, vel per Harmoniam Praestabilitam* (London, 1769)

Printed in the United States of America

ISBN (library)	978-0-87785-507-1
ISBN (e-book of library edition)	978-0-87785-717-4
ISBN (Portable)	**978-0-87785-434-0**
ISBN (e-book of Portable Edition)	978-0-87785-716-7

Library of Congress Cataloging-in-Publication Data

Names: Swedenborg, Emanuel, 1688–1772, author. | Rose, Jonathan S., 1956–, translator. | Dole, George F., translator. | Swedenborg, Emanuel, 1688–1772. Summaria expositio doctrinae Novae Ecclesiae, quae per Novam Hierosolymam in Apocalypsi intelligitur. English. | Swedenborg, Emanuel, 1688–1772. De commercio animae et corporis. English.
Title: Survey ; Soul-body interaction / Emanuel Swedenborg.
Other titles: Soul-body interaction
Description: The portable New Century edition. | West Chester, Pennsylvania : Swedenborg Foundation, 2022 | "The Portable New Century edition of Emanuel Swedenborg's Survey, translated from the Latin by Jonathan S. Rose, and Soul-body interaction, translated from the Latin by George F. Dole." | Summary: "These two shorter works by Swedish theologian Emanuel Swedenborg (1688–1772), originally published separately and very different in content, both represent Swedenborg's own effort to summarize complex areas of his thought. In Survey, Swedenborg discusses some key tenets of Christian doctrine, both Catholic and Protestant, and describes how his own theology differs from it. In Soul-Body Interaction, he takes as his subject the way life flows from the transcendent God into all living things"— Provided by publisher.
Identifiers: LCCN 2021016512 | ISBN 9780877854340 (paperback) | ISBN 9780877857167 (epub)
Subjects: LCSH: New Jerusalem Church—Doctrines. | Mind and body—Early works to 1800. | Cosmology—Early works to 1800.
Classification: LCC BX8711.A7 R668 2022 | DDC 233/.5—dc23
LC record available at https://lccn.loc.gov/2021016512

Senior copy editor, Alicia L. Dole
Text designed by Joanna V. Hill
Ornaments from the first Latin editions, 1769
Typesetting by Alicia L. Dole, Mary M. Wachsmann, and Sarah Dole
Cover designed by Karen Connor
Cover photograph by Daniel Petzold / EyeEm

For information contact:
Swedenborg Foundation
320 North Church Street
West Chester, PA 19380 USA
Telephone: (610) 430-3222
Web: www.swedenborg.com
E-mail: info@swedenborg.com

Contents

1. §§17–18 / The churches that separated from Roman Catholicism
   during the Reformation disagree with each other on many points
   of theology, but there are four points on which they all agree: there
   is a trinity of persons in the Divine; original sin came from Adam;
   Christ's merit is assigned to us; and we are justified by faith alone.   19

2. §§19–20 / In fact, in regard to the four theological points just
   listed, Roman Catholics before the Reformation had exactly the same
   teachings as Protestants did after it. That is, Catholics had the
   same teachings regarding the trinity of persons in the Divine,
   the same teachings regarding original sin, the same teachings regarding
   the assigning of Christ's merit, and the same teachings regarding our
   being justified by believing that we are assigned Christ's merit; the
   only difference was that Catholics united that faith to goodwill or
   good works.   20

3. §§21–23 / The leading reformers—Luther, Melanchthon, and
   Calvin—retained all the dogmas regarding the trinity of persons
   in the Divine, original sin, the assigning of Christ's merit to us,
   and our being justified by faith, in the same past and present form
   they had had among Roman Catholics. The reformers separated
   goodwill or good works from that faith, however, and declared
   that our good works contribute nothing to our salvation, for the

Soul-Body Interaction

Editors' Preface

JONATHAN S. ROSE
and
STUART SHOTWELL

T HE two works in this volume, Swedenborg's *Survey* and *Soul-Body Interaction,* have not previously been bound together except when they appeared with other short works in compendium volumes; that is, they have not been joined as the sole contents of a single volume. Given their apparently disparate nature, it seems necessary to explain why they appear together here.

It was the plan of the original New Century Edition Editorial Committee that readers of the entire hardcover set would be able to place the volumes of the series on their shelves in the order in which Swedenborg published them. Such a physical arrangement on the shelves, while certainly not critical to appreciating Swedenborg's theology and philosophy, would nevertheless conduce, over time, to the reader's understanding of what Swedenborg wrote when and why. Since the two works in this combination volume were originally published in 1769, they deserve to stand next to one another in the New Century Edition on that basis alone; and given their short length, each gains physical heft, at least, through the support of the other.

However, there are other and less material benefits from their inclusion together. *Survey* and *Soul-Body Interaction* complement each other in challenging what Swedenborg viewed as common misconceptions in contemporary thought. *Survey* focuses on theology, while *Soul-Body Interaction* addresses philosophical thought, which at that time also encompassed science.

The two works are, furthermore, oddly compatible as mirroring pieces in one other respect: *Survey* was written to be a preview of the final work of Swedenborg's career, *True Christianity,* which he brought to completion in 1771; whereas *Soul-Body Interaction* was Swedenborg's final word on a topic on which he had written several times in various contexts over his long and productive life. *Survey* might then be called a blueprint for a larger work, and *Soul-Body Interaction* the final edifice resulting from several blueprints.

Conventions Used in This Work

SURVEY and *Soul-Body Interaction* were originally published separately in 1769. For introductory material on the content and history of *Survey* and *Soul-Body Interaction,* and for annotations on their subject matter, with an extensive index, the reader is referred to the Deluxe New Century Edition volume. In general, the introductions in this series discuss the key ideas presented in each work, as well as the relationship of those ideas to the history of ideas, and specifically to their eighteenth-century context. The subsequent influence of the works is also treated. The annotations provide definitions of unfamiliar terms; clarification of direct or indirect references to people, places, events, or other works; and information on matters that present challenges to current readers because of changes in culture over time.

Section numbers Following a practice common in his time, Swedenborg divided his published theological works into sections numbered in sequence from beginning to end. His original section numbers have been preserved in this edition; they appear in boxes in the outside margins. Traditionally, these sections have been referred to as "numbers" and designated by the abbreviation "n." In this edition, however, the more common section symbol (§) is used to designate the section numbers, and the sections are referred to as such.

Subsection numbers Because many sections throughout Swedenborg's works are too long for precise cross-referencing, Swedenborgian scholar John Faulkner Potts (1838–1923) further divided them into subsections; these have since become standard, though minor variations occur from one edition to another. These subsections are indicated by bracketed numbers that appear in the text itself: [2], [3], and so on. Because the beginning of the first *subsection* always coincides with the beginning of the *section* proper, it is not labeled in the text.

Citations of Swedenborg's text As is common in Swedenborgian studies, text citations of Swedenborg's works refer not to page numbers but to section numbers, which unlike page numbers are uniform in most editions. In citations the section symbol (§) is generally omitted after the title of a work by Swedenborg. Thus "*Revelation Unveiled* 529" would refer to section 529 (§529) of Swedenborg's *Revelation Unveiled,* not to page 529 of any edition. Subsection numbers are given after a colon; a reference such as "529:2" indicates subsection 2 of section 529. The reference "529:1" would indicate the first subsection of section 529, though that subsection is not in fact labeled in the text. Where section numbers stand alone without titles, their function is indicated by the prefixed section symbol; for example, "§529:2".

Citations of the Bible Biblical citations in this edition follow the accepted standard: a semicolon is used between book references and between chapter references, and a comma between verse references. Therefore "Matthew 5:11, 12; 6:1; 10:41, 42; Luke 6:23, 35" refers to Matthew chapter 5, verses 11 and 12; Matthew chapter 6, verse 1; Matthew chapter 10, verses 41 and 42; and Luke chapter 6, verses 23 and 35. Swedenborg often incorporated the numbers of verses not actually represented in his text when listing verse numbers for a passage he quoted; these apparently constitute a kind of "see also" reference to other material he felt was relevant, and are generally retained in this edition. This edition also follows Swedenborg where he cites contiguous verses individually (for example, John 14:8, 9, 10, 11), rather than as a range (John 14:8–11). Occasionally this edition supplies a full, conventional Bible reference where Swedenborg omits one after a quotation.

Quotations in Swedenborg's works Some features of the original Latin texts have been modernized in this edition. For example, Swedenborg's first edition often relies on context or italics rather than on quotation marks to indicate passages taken from the Bible or from other works. The manner in which these conventions are used in the original suggests that Swedenborg did not feel it necessary to belabor the distinction between direct quotation and paraphrase; neither did he mark his omissions from or changes to material he quoted, a practice in which this edition generally follows him.

Italicized terms Any words in indented scriptural extracts that are here set in italics reflect a similar emphasis in the first edition.

Special use of vertical rule The author's appendix to *Survey* (§§116–117) is set in large type in the first edition. In this edition this passage is marked by a vertical rule in the margin.

Changes to and insertions in the text This translation is based on the first Latin editions, published by Swedenborg himself. It incorporates the silent emendation of minor errors, not only in the text proper but in Bible verse references and in section references to Swedenborg's other published theological works. The text has also been changed without notice where the verse numbering of the Latin Bible cited by Swedenborg differs from that of modern English Bibles. Throughout the translation, references or cross-references that were implied but not stated have been inserted in square brackets []; for example, [Matthew 18:20]. Occasionally such brackets represent an insertion of material that was not present in the first edition, but no annotation concerning these insertions is supplied in this Portable edition. By contrast, references that occur in parentheses reflect references that appear in the first edition; for example, (John 7:39), (see §§39, 40). Words not occurring in the first Latin edition, but necessary for the understanding of the text, also appear in square brackets; this device has been used sparingly, however, even at the risk of some inconsistency in its application.

Biblical titles Swedenborg refers to the Hebrew Scriptures as the Old Testament and to the Greek Scriptures as the New Testament; his terminology has been adopted in this edition.

Survey

of Teachings of

the New Church

Meant by

the New Jerusalem

in

the Book of Revelation

By Emanuel Swedenborg
A Swede

Revelation 21:2, 5

I, John, saw the holy city, the new Jerusalem, coming down from God out of heaven, prepared as a bride adorned for her husband. And the one sitting on the throne said, "Behold, I am making all things new"; and said to me, "Write, because these words are true and trustworthy."

Survey of Teachings
of the New Church
Meant by the New Jerusalem
in the Book of Revelation

[Author's Preface]

AFTER publishing, within the span of a few years, several larger and smaller works on the *New Jerusalem* (which means the new church that the Lord is going to establish), and after unveiling the Book of Revelation, I resolved to publish and bring to light the teachings of the [new] church in their fullness, and thus to present a body of teaching that was whole. But because this work was going to take several years, I developed a plan to publish an outline of it, to give people an initial, general picture of this church and its teachings. When a general overview precedes, all the details that follow, of however wide a range, stand forth in a clear light, because they each have their own place within the overall structure alongside things of the same type.

This briefing does not include detailed argumentation; it is shared as advance notice, because the points it contains will be fully demonstrated in the work itself.

First, however, I must present the teachings concerning justification as they exist today, in order to highlight the differences between the tenets of today's church and those of the new church.

Roman Catholic Teachings Concerning Justification, Taken from the Council of Trent

2 In the papal bull issued by the Roman pope Pius IV on November 13, 1564, we read the following:

> I embrace and accept each and every thing that has been defined and declared by *the holy Council of Trent* concerning *original sin* and *justification*.

3 From *the Council of Trent concerning original sin:*
(a) The entire Adam, through the offense of his prevarication, was changed, in body and soul, for the worse. The prevarication of Adam injured not only himself but also his posterity; it transfused not only death and pains of the body into the whole human race but also sin itself, which is the death of the soul (Session 5, numbers 1, 2).

(b) This sin of Adam—which in its origin is one, and being transfused by propagation, not by imitation, is in each one as his or her own—cannot be taken away by any other remedy than the merit of the one and only Savior, our Lord Jesus Christ, who reconciled us to God in his own blood, being made justice, sanctification, and redemption for us (Session 5, number 3).

(c) All human beings had lost their innocence in the prevarication of Adam; they became unclean and by nature children of wrath (Session 6, chapter 1).

4 *Concerning justification:*
(a) When that blessed fullness of time had come, the heavenly Father, the Father of mercies, sent Jesus Christ, his own Son, to the human race, in order both to [redeem] the Jews, who were under the law, and to allow the Gentiles, who were not following justice, to attain it, and all people to receive adoption as his children. God sent him forth as a propitiator for

our sins through faith in his blood, not for our sins only but also for those of the whole world (Session 6, chapter 2).

(b) Nevertheless, not all people receive the benefit of Christ's death, but only those with whom he shares the merit earned through his suffering. Therefore if people were not born again in Christ, they never would be justified (Session 6, chapter 3).

(c) The beginning of this justification is to be derived from the pre-existing grace of God through Jesus Christ, that is, from his calling to us (Session 6, chapter 5).

(d) We are made ready for his justice when, stirred by divine grace and conceiving faith by hearing, we freely move toward God, believing those things to be true that have been divinely revealed and promised to us—especially this promise, that God justifies the impious by his grace, through the redemption that is in Christ Jesus, and that when we understand that we are sinners and are beneficially struck with fear of divine justice, we are raised to hope since we have confidence that God is appeased toward us because of Christ (Session 6, chapter 6).

(e) This readiness and preparation are followed by the process itself of being justified, which is not only a forgiving of our sins but also a sanctification and renewal of our inner self through the receiving of the grace and of the gifts by which we turn from an unjust person into a just person and from an enemy [of God] into a friend, so that we inherit the hope of everlasting life (Session 6, chapter 7).

(f) The *final cause* of this justification is the glory of God and of Christ, and life everlasting. The *efficient cause* is a merciful God who washes and sanctifies us gratuitously. The *meritorious cause* is God's most beloved Only-Begotten, our Lord Jesus Christ, who, when we were enemies, for the exceeding goodwill with which he loved us, merited justification for us by his most holy suffering on the wood of the cross, and made satisfaction for us to God the Father. The *instrumental cause* is the sacrament of baptism, which is the sacrament of the faith without which no one was ever justified. The lone *formal cause* is the justice of God—not the justice with which he himself is just, but the justice with which he makes us just; namely, the justice with which we, being endowed by him, are renewed in the spirit of our mind, and we are not only reputed just, but are truly called just, and are in fact just, receiving justice within us, each according to our own measure, which the Holy Spirit distributes to everyone as he wills (Session 6, chapter 7, §2).

(g) Justification is a transferal from that state in which we are born a child of the first Adam, to the state of grace and our adoption as children of God through the second Adam, Jesus Christ our Savior (Session 6, chapter 4).

5 *Concerning faith, goodwill, good works, and rewards:*
(a) When the apostle says that we are justified by faith and we are justified freely [Romans 3:24, 28], these words are to be understood in the sense that the perpetual consent of the Catholic Church has held and expressed: namely, that we are said to be justified by faith because faith is the beginning of human salvation, and the foundation and root of all justification. Without faith, it is impossible to please God and to come into the company of his children. We are said to be justified freely because none of the things that precede justification—whether faith or works—merit the grace itself of justification. If it is by grace, then it is not by works; otherwise grace would not be grace (Session 6, chapter 8).

(b) Although no one can be just except those with whom the rewards for the suffering of our Lord Jesus Christ are shared, this does in fact happen in the process of justification, when by the merit of that same most holy suffering, the goodwill of God is poured forth by the Holy Spirit into the hearts of those who are justified, and becomes inherent in them. As a result, as we are justified and our sins are forgiven, we receive all these [gifts] infused at once through Jesus Christ, onto whom we are grafted through faith, hope, and goodwill. Unless goodwill is added to it, faith does not unite us perfectly with Christ, and does not make us a living member of his body (Session 6, chapter 7, §3).

(c) Christ is not only a redeemer in whom we are to trust but also a legislator whom we are to obey (Session 6, chapter 16, canon 21).

(d) Faith without works is dead and profitless, because in Christ Jesus neither circumcision nor uncircumcision avails anything, but faith that works through goodwill. Faith without hope and goodwill cannot bestow everlasting life. As a result, we immediately hear these words of Christ: "If you will enter into life, keep the commandments." Therefore, when receiving true and Christian justice, we are told, immediately upon being born again, to preserve it pure and spotless, as the first robe given us through Jesus Christ in lieu of the robe that Adam, by his disobedience, lost for himself and for us, so that we may bear it before the judgment-seat of our Lord Jesus Christ and have life everlasting (Session 6, chapter 7, §4).

(e) As the head into the members and the vine into the branches, Jesus Christ himself continually infuses his virtue into those who have been justified. This virtue always precedes and accompanies and follows our good works; without it they could not in any way be pleasing or meritorious before God. Therefore we must believe that for the justified nothing further is lacking that would in any way diminish their being considered, by the works they have done in God, as deserving of eternal life in due time (Session 6, chapter 16).

(f) Our own justice is therefore not established as our own, as from ourselves; for the justice that is called ours actually belongs to God, because it is infused into us by God through the merit of Christ. Nevertheless God forbid that Christians should either trust or glory in themselves and not in the Lord, whose bounty toward all is so great that he wants things that are his own gifts to be their rewards (Session 6, chapter 16).

(g) We can do nothing of ourselves, as of ourselves; but with the cooperation of him who strengthens us, we can do all things. Therefore we have nothing in which to glory; all our glory is in Christ in whom we live, by whom we merit, and by whom we make satisfaction, bringing forth fruits worthy of repentance, which have their efficacy from him, are offered to the Father by him, and are accepted by the Father through him (Session 14, chapter 8).

(h) If any say that we can be justified before God by our own works (whether done through the power of our own human nature or through following the teaching of the law) without the grace of God through Jesus Christ, let them be anathema (Session 6, canon 1).

(i) If any say that without previous inspiration of the Holy Spirit, and without his help, we can believe, hope, or love [that is, have faith, hope, or goodwill] as we ought, so that the grace of justification may be bestowed upon us, let them be anathema (Session 6, canon 3).

(j) If any say that we can be made just without the justice of Christ through which he gained merit for us, let them be anathema (Session 6, canon 10).

There are many other statements there that could be quoted as well, especially concerning the union of faith and goodwill or good works, and the damnation that comes of separating these two.

Concerning free choice:

(a) Free choice was by no means extinguished by Adam's sin, but was attenuated in its powers and bent down (Session 6, chapter 1).

6

(b) If any say that our free choice, once it is moved and stirred by God, does not cooperate at all through giving assent to God's stirring and calling, in order to dispose and prepare us for obtaining the grace of justification, or that even if it wants to, it cannot refuse its consent, but, like something inanimate, does nothing whatever and is merely passive, let them be anathema (Session 6, canon 4).

7 *The teachings of the Roman Catholics on justification, as gathered from the decrees of the Council of Trent, can be linked together and summed up as follows:*

The sin of Adam was transfused into the entire human race. As a result, the state of the human race and of every individual within it was ruined and alienated from God. People became enemies [of God] and children of wrath. Therefore God the Father as an act of grace sent his Son to reconcile, ritually purge, appease, make satisfaction, and thereby redeem; and to do so by becoming justice.

Christ carried out and fulfilled this task by offering himself to God the Father as a sacrifice on the wood of the cross, that is, through his own suffering and his own blood. Christ alone earned merit. God the Father through the agency of the Holy Spirit assigns, attributes, applies, and transfers this merit of Christ's to receptive individuals as an act of grace. In this way the sin of Adam is removed from them, although cravings do nonetheless remain and entice them to sin.

Justification is the forgiving of sins, which leads to a renewal of the inner self, by which we turn from an enemy [of God] into a friend and from a child of wrath into a child of grace. This brings us into a union with Christ. We are reborn as a living part of his body.

8 Faith comes to us through hearing, when we believe that the teachings divinely revealed to us are true and when we trust in God's promises. Faith is the beginning of human salvation, and the foundation and root of all justification. Without faith, it is impossible to please God and to come into the company of his children. Our justification takes place through faith, hope, and goodwill. Unless hope and goodwill are added to faith, it is dead rather than living and does not unite us to Christ.

We need to cooperate in this process. We have the power to move either closer to or farther away from [Christ]; if we did not, nothing could be granted to us, because we would be like a lifeless body.

Our openness to being justified renews us; this renewal takes place as Christ's merit is applied to us, as the result of our own cooperation. Therefore we get credit for the works that we do; yet because they are done as a result of grace and through the Holy Spirit, and because Christ alone has earned merit, the rewards God gives us are his own gifts within us. Therefore none of us can attribute anything of merit to ourselves.

Protestant Teachings Concerning Justification, Taken from the *Formula of Concord*

The book that is the source of the following statements is called the **9** *Formula of Concord;* it was written by people who endorsed the Augsburg Confession. Because I will be giving the page numbers from which these statements were taken, I should mention that what I am citing is the Leipzig edition of 1756.

Teachings from the Formula of Concord *on original sin:*   **10**
(a) Since the fall of Adam, all human beings who are propagated according to nature are born with sin, which condemns and brings eternal death to those who are not born anew. The merit of Christ is the sole means and instrument through which we are reborn, and therefore the only remedy by which we are healed (pages 9, 10, 52, 53, 55, 317, 641, 644, and the appendix, pages 138, 139).

(b) Original sin is a corruption of our nature at such a deep level that there is nothing spiritually sound left in the human body or soul or in their powers (page 574).

(c) It is the source of all other, actual sins (pages 317, 577, 639, 640, 942; appendix, page 139).

(d) It is the complete absence or lack of the image of God (page 640).

(e) A distinction must be maintained between our nature, as it was created by God, and the original sin that resides within our nature (page 645).

(f) The volume refers to original sin as the Devil's work, spiritual poison, and the root of all evils, and says it is an "accident" and a "quality." Our nature, on the other hand, is there referred to as the work and the creation of God; it is our person, substance, and essence. The volume gives as a comparison the distinction between the person who is infected with a disease and the disease itself.

11 *Teachings on justification by faith.* The *general teachings* of the volume are as follows.

(a) Through the Word and the sacraments the Holy Spirit is given, who produces faith where and when he wills in those who hear the gospel.

(b) Contrition, justification by faith, renewal, and good works follow each other in sequence. It is of great importance to differentiate between them, however. Contrition and good works contribute nothing to our salvation; faith alone saves.

(c) Justification by faith alone is the forgiving of our sins, absolution from damnation, reconciliation with the Father, and adoption as his children. This is accomplished through the assignment to us of the merit or righteousness of Christ.

(d) Therefore faith is the righteousness itself by which we are considered to be just before God. Faith is confidence and trust in grace.

(e) Our renewal, which follows our justification, is our being brought to life, regenerated, and sanctified.

(f) Good works follow this renewal. They are the fruits of faith, and are actually works of the Spirit.

(g) We lose this faith if we commit serious evils.
The following are *general teachings concerning the law and the gospel:*

(h) It is important to differentiate between the law and the gospel, and between the works of the law and the works of the Spirit, which are the fruits of faith.

(i) The law is the teaching that shows us we have sins and are therefore in a state of damnation and under the wrath of God; this terrifies us. The gospel is the teaching about how we are ritually purged from sin and damnation by Christ; it is the teaching that comforts us.

(j) The law has three functions: to restrain the ungodly; to lead people to recognize their sins; and to teach the reborn the rules of life.

(k) The reborn live and walk in the law, but they are not under the law; they are under grace.

(l) The reborn should practice following what the law teaches, because as long as they are still living in this world, they are urged by their flesh to sin; after death, however, they become pure and perfect.

(m) Even the reborn struggle with the Holy Spirit and resist it in various ways. Nevertheless, they willingly obey the law and therefore live in the law as children of God.

(n) In those who are not reborn, the veil of Moses remains in front of the eyes and the old Adam is dominant. In those who are reborn, the veil of Moses is taken away and the old Adam is repeatedly put to death.

Particular teachings from the Formula of Concord *concerning our being justified by faith apart from the works of the law:*

(a) Faith is attributed to us as righteousness apart from the works of the law, because of the merit of Christ that faith brings us (pages 78, 79, 80, 584, 689).

(b) Goodwill comes along only after we have the faith that makes us just. Faith actually does not make us just if it has been formed through acts of goodwill, although Catholics say it does (pages 81, 89, 94, 117, 688, 691; appendix, page 169).

(c) The contrition that precedes, and the renewal, sanctification, and good works that follow, have no part to play in the business of being justified by faith (pages 688, 689).

(d) It is foolish to dream that the works enjoined by the second tablet of the Ten Commandments make us just before God. We follow them in our dealings with other human beings, but not with God. In the process of being justified we must deal with God and placate his wrath (page 102).

(e) Any who believe their sins are forgiven because they do acts of goodwill are insulting Christ; their confidence in their own righteousness is wicked and futile (pages 87, 89).

(f) Good works must be completely excluded from any discussion of our justification and eternal life (page 589).

(g) Good works are not necessary to make us deserving of salvation; they play no part in activating the process of being justified (pages 589, 590, 702, 704; appendix, page 173).

(h) We must reject the proposition that good works are necessary for our salvation. This position takes away the consolation of the gospel, gives us a reason to doubt God's grace, and strengthens the presumption that we ourselves are righteous. Papists adopted these views in support of a bad cause (page 704).

(i) We reject and condemn the expression that good works are necessary for salvation (page 591).

(j) Statements that good works are necessary for salvation are not to be taught or defended, but should be excluded and rejected by our churches as false (page 705).

(k) Works that do not proceed from true faith are actually sins in God's sight. That is, such works are tarnished with sin, since a bad tree cannot bear good fruit (page 700).

(l) Our good works do not preserve or maintain faith or salvation in us; they are just a testimony that the Holy Spirit is present and dwelling within us (pages 590, 705; appendix, page 174).

(m) People ought to reject the decree of the Council of Trent [and whatever else is used to support the opinion] that our good works preserve salvation or that our works either completely or only in part preserve and maintain the righteousness received by faith or even faith itself (page 707).

13 *Particular teachings from the* Formula of Concord *concerning the fruits of faith:*

(a) The difference between the works of the law and the works of the Spirit must be most diligently noted. The works that the reborn do with a free and joyful spirit are not works of the law but works of the Spirit; they are the fruits of faith. Such people are no longer under the law but under grace (pages 589, 590, 721, 722).

(b) Good works are the fruits of repentance (page 12).

(c) Through faith, the reborn receive a new life, new desires, and new works; these come from the faith that exists in repentance (page 134).

(d) After this conversion and justification, our minds and eventually even our intellects begin to be renewed. Then our will is not idle in the daily exercise of repentance (pages 582, 673, 700).

(e) We need to practice repentance both from original sin and from our own actual sins (page 321; appendix, page 159).

(f) This repentance endures among Christians until death because it struggles with the sin that remains in the flesh throughout life (page 327).

(g) The law of the Ten Commandments must take hold in us and then increase more and more (pages 85, 86).

(h) Although the reborn are indeed liberated from the curse of the law, they should daily practice the law of the Lord (page 718).

(i) The reborn are never without the law, and at the same time they are not under the law; they live according to the law of the Lord (page 722).

(j) For those who are reborn, the law must be the norm of their religious practice (pages 596, 717; appendix, page 156).

(k) The reborn do good works not by coercion but spontaneously and freely, as if they knew of no commandment, had heard no threat, and were expecting no reward (pages 596, 701).

(l) The faith the reborn have is constantly engaged in doing good works. Whoever does not do such works is an unbeliever. Where faith exists, there good works are being done (page 701).

(m) Goodwill and worthy fruits follow faith and regeneration (pages 121, 122, 171, 188, 692).

(n) Faith and good works fit beautifully together and are inseparably connected. But it is faith alone that lays hold of the blessing, apart from works, and yet it is never, ever alone. As a result, faith without works is dead (pages 692, 693).

(o) After a person has been justified by faith, there then exists a true, living faith that works through love. Good works always follow justifying faith and are certainly found with it. Faith is never alone but is always accompanied by love and hope (page 586).

(p) We say that if good works do not follow, then faith is false and not true (page 336).

(q) It is impossible to separate good works from faith, quite as impossible as to separate heat and light from fire (page 701).

(r) Because the old Adam still continues to hang on in their nature, the reborn need not only the law's daily instruction and admonition, its warning and threatening; often they also need its punishments. They are reproved and restrained by the Holy Spirit through the law (pages 719, 720, 721).

(s) The reborn still have to struggle with the old Adam. The flesh, which is still a part of them, needs to be forced into obedience through admonitions, threats, and blows, since the renewal of life through faith merely begins in this lifetime (pages 595, 596, 724).

(t) The battle of the flesh against the Spirit continues even in the elect and truly reborn (pages 675, 679).

(u) Christ announces that our sins will be forgiven because of our good works. He says this for three reasons: because our good works follow our being reconciled to God; because good fruits ought of necessity to follow [our repentance]; and because our good works are signs of his promise to us (pages 116, 117).

(v) There is no saving faith in those who lack goodwill. Love is a fruit that certainly and necessarily results from true faith (page 688).

(w) Good works are necessary for a host of reasons, but we are not to count on meriting [grace] through them (pages 11, 17, 64, 95, 133, 589, 590, 702; appendix, page 172).

(x) With the new powers and gifts the reborn have received, they should cooperate with the Holy Spirit, but in a particular way (pages 582, 583, 674, 675; appendix, page 144).

(y) In the Belgic Confession, which was officially adopted at the Synod of Dort, we read the following:

> It is impossible for this holy faith to be unfruitful in us—faith works through love. These works, as they proceed from the good root of faith, are good and acceptable in the sight of God, like the fruit of a good tree. We are indebted to God for the good works we do, but he is not indebted to us on their account, since it is he who produces them in us. (Belgic Confession [24])

14 *Teachings from the* Formula of Concord *on merit:*

(a) It is false that we merit the forgiveness of sins through our works. It is false that we are counted righteous because of the righteousness of our reason. It is false that reason by its own powers is able to love God above all things and to fulfill God's law (page 64).

(b) Faith does not make people righteous because it is such a good work or such a fine virtue, but because it lays hold of and accepts the merit of Christ in the promise of the holy gospel (pages 76, 684).

(c) The promise of the forgiveness of sins and of being made righteous on account of Christ is not conditional upon our merits; it is offered for free (page 67).

(d) We sinful people are justified before God, that is, absolved of our sins and of the judgment of damnation that we deserve, and we are accepted as children and heirs of God, without the least bit of our own merit, apart from all preceding, present, or subsequent works that we do. We are justified on the basis of sheer grace, because of the sole merit of Christ, which is reckoned to us as righteousness (page 684).

(e) Good works follow faith, forgiveness of sins, and regeneration. Whatever in these works is still sinful or imperfect should not even be counted as sin or imperfection, precisely for the sake of this same Christ. Instead, we should be called, and should be, completely righteous and holy—both we ourselves and the works we do—by the pure grace and mercy that have been poured and spread over us in Christ. Therefore we cannot boast about our merit (pages 74, 92, 93, 336).

(f) Those who trust that they merit grace by works despise the merit and grace of Christ and seek a way to heaven through human powers alone without Christ (pages 16, 17, 18, 19).

(g) If people want to mix good works up with the article on justification and want to merit God's grace through them, works are not only useless for such people but even harmful (page 708).

(h) The works of the Ten Commandments are listed, and many other things that must be done; God honors these works with rewards (pages 176, 198).

(i) We concede that works are truly meritorious, but not for the forgiveness of sins, for grace, or for justification. Works are meritorious for other bodily and spiritual rewards, which are bestowed both in this life and in the life to come. According to the passage in Paul, "Each will receive wages according to the labor of each"; and Christ says, "Your reward will be great in heaven." Christ often says that he will repay according to each one's deeds. We confess, therefore, that eternal life is a reward, because it is owed to the justified on account of the promise, and because God crowns his gifts, but not because of our merit (pages 96, 133, 134, 135, 136, 137, 138).

(j) Good works in believers are an indication of their eternal salvation when these are done for the right reasons and the right purposes (that is, in the way God demands the reborn to do them). God the Father holds these works as well received and pleasing for Christ's sake and promises a glorious reward for them in this life and in the life to come (page 708).

(k) Although good works deserve rewards, nevertheless neither by merit of fitness nor by merit of agreement do they earn us forgiveness of sins or the glory of eternal life (pages 96, 135, 139 and following; appendix, page 174).

(l) In the Last Judgment, Christ is going to hand down a sentence regarding which works were good or evil depending on whether those works were the genuine result of, and are evidence for, people's faith (page 134; appendix, page 187).

(m) God does reward good works, but it is because of his grace that he crowns them, since they were actually gifts from him (Belgic Confession [24]).

Teachings from the Formula of Concord *on free choice:*

(a) Human beings are completely powerless in spiritual matters (pages 15, 18, 219, 318, 579, 656 and following; appendix, page 141).

(b) We human beings have been so deeply corrupted through the fall of our first parents that in spiritual matters concerning our conversion and salvation we are by nature blind. We regard the Word of God as foolishness. We are an enemy of God, and remain so until from pure grace without any cooperation on our part we are converted, given faith, regenerated, and renewed by the power of the Holy Spirit through the Word as it is preached and heard (pages 656, 657).

(c) We are utterly corrupt and dead to what is good, so that in our nature after the Fall but before our regeneration not the least spark of spiritual power remains that would enable us to prepare ourselves for the grace of God, or accept it once it was offered, or make room for it by ourselves or on our own. In spiritual matters, we are entirely unable to understand, believe, comprehend, think, will, start, finish, enact, work, or cooperate through our own natural powers, or adapt or accommodate ourselves to grace or contribute anything to our own conversion in whole or by half or to the least extent by acting on our own (pages 656, 658).

(d) In spiritual and divine matters, which concern the soul's salvation, the human being is like a pillar of salt, like Lot's wife, and indeed like a lifeless block of wood or a stone, which has no eyes or mouth or senses (pages 661, 662).

(e) Although people have the power to move their bodies and control their limbs and can attend public worship and hear the Word and the gospel, they nevertheless regard those things as foolishness in their silent thoughts. In this sense they are worse than a block of wood, if the Holy Spirit does not become active in them (pages 662, 671, 672, 673).

(f) As we undergo conversion, it happens not as a statue is formed in stone or a seal is pressed in wax; these things do not know or feel or will anything (pages 662, 681).

(g) In our conversion we are "purely passive" and not active at all (pages 662, 681).

(h) In our conversion, we do not cooperate with the Holy Spirit at all (pages 219, 579, 583, 672, 676; appendix, pages 143, 144).

(i) Since the Fall, human beings have retained and still possess earthly powers of knowledge, as well as free choice (to some extent at least) in choosing what is good on an earthly and civic level (pages 14, 218, 641, 664; appendix, page 142).

(j) Some ancient and modern teachers of the church have used expressions such as "God draws, but he draws the willing"; we hold that these expressions do not correspond to the form of sound teaching (pages 582, 583).

(k) Using power from the Holy Spirit, the reborn cooperate with him, though still in great weakness. This occurs on the basis of the new powers and gifts that the Holy Spirit initiated in us in conversion. This leading of the Holy Spirit is not a compulsion; rather, the converted person does good things spontaneously (pages 582 and following, 673, 674, 675; appendix, page 144).

(l) It is not just the gifts of God that reside in the reborn, but because of their faith, Christ too dwells in them as in his temple (pages 695, 697, 698; appendix, page 130).

(m) There is a great difference between baptized and unbaptized people. According to Paul's teaching, "All those who have been baptized have put on Christ," and are therefore truly reborn. They now have a "freed choice"; that is, as Christ says, "They have been made free again." For this reason they not only hear the Word of God but are also able to assent to it and embrace it with faith—although in great weakness (page 675).

It is important to note that the preceding quotations were taken from the book called the *Formula of Concord,* which was written by people who endorsed the Augsburg Confession. Nevertheless, the same things regarding justification by faith alone are said and taught by Protestants in Britain and the Netherlands as well. Therefore the statements that follow are intended for all. See also §§17, 18 just below.

Sketch of the Teachings of the New Church

16 WHAT follows here is a survey of the teachings of the new church meant by the New Jerusalem in Revelation 21 and 22. In the work itself, these teachings, which concern not only what to believe but also how to live, will be broken into three parts.

Part 1 will present teachings on the following topics:

1. The Lord God the Savior, and the Divine Trinity within Him
2. Sacred Scripture; Its Two Meanings, Earthly and Spiritual; and Its Resulting Holiness
3. Love for God, Love for Our Neighbor, and the Harmony between Them
4. Faith, and Its Partnership with Those Two Types of Love
5. Teachings about Life Drawn from the Ten Commandments
6. Reformation and Regeneration
7. Free Choice, and Our Cooperation with the Lord by Means of It
8. Baptism
9. The Holy Supper
10. Heaven and Hell
11. Our Partnership with Heaven or Hell, and How Our State of Life after Death Depends on That Partnership
12. Eternal Life

Part 2 will discuss the following topics:

1. The Close of the Age, the End of the Church in Existence Today
2. The Coming of the Lord
3. The Last Judgment
4. The New Church, Which Is the New Jerusalem

Part 3 will demonstrate *the discordance* between the tenets of the church in existence today and those of the new church.

In the present volume, too, we will spend a little time on these points of discordance, because both clergy and lay people in the church of today believe that their church is walking in the very light of the gospel and in truths that cannot be weakened, uprooted, or assailed, even by an angel, if one should come down from heaven. The church today cannot see otherwise, because it has withdrawn the intellect from matters of faith, and has supported its tenets through a kind of sight that exists beneath the intellect. That level [of the mind] is able to provide argumentation to support falsities so effectively that they appear to be truths. Once falsities have been reinforced on that level, they gain a deceptive kind of light. Where light of that kind exists, the light of truths looks like thick darkness.

For this reason we will spend a little time presenting points of discordance, and noting a few things about them by way of illustration, so that people whose intellects have not been closed off by blind faith will be able to see the differences, first as in twilight, then as in morning light, and eventually (when the work itself appears) as in the full light of day.

In general, the points of discordance are the following.

I

The churches that separated from Roman Catholicism during the Reformation disagree with each other on many points of theology, but there are four points on which they all agree: there is a trinity of persons in the Divine; original sin came from Adam; Christ's merit is assigned to us; and we are justified by faith alone.   **17**

Brief Analysis

The churches that separated from Roman Catholicism during the Reformation consist of those who call themselves Evangelicals and those who call themselves the Reformed and also Protestants, and who are named Lutherans or Calvinists after the founders of their churches. The Anglican Church holds middle ground between them. (I am not referring here to the Orthodox churches, which separated from Roman Catholicism a long time ago.)   **18**

Many people are aware that the Protestant churches have theological disagreements with each other in a number of areas—especially concerning the Holy Supper, baptism, the person of Christ, and the process whereby people become "the chosen."

It is not widely recognized, however, that there are four points on which all these churches agree: there is a trinity of persons in the Divine; there is such a thing as original sin; Christ's merit is assigned to us; and we are justified by faith alone. The reason this is not widely recognized is that few people conduct research on the dogmatic differences between the churches, and therefore few realize the points the churches have in common. Members of the clergy limit themselves to an investigation of the tenets of their own church; and lay people rarely examine those tenets deeply enough to see the differences and similarities.

Nevertheless, on these four points, Protestants do agree, both generally and in most of the details, as you will find if you consult their books and listen to their sermons. (This point is established first for the sake of the points that are about to follow.)

2

19 *In fact, in regard to the four theological points just listed, Roman Catholics before the Reformation had exactly the same teachings as Protestants did after it. That is, Catholics had the same teachings regarding the trinity of persons in the Divine, the same teachings regarding original sin, the same teachings regarding the assigning of Christ's merit, and the same teachings regarding our being justified by believing that we are assigned Christ's merit; the only difference was that Catholics united that faith to goodwill or good works.*

Brief Analysis

20 Although scarcely anyone has realized it, on these four points Protestants agree with Roman Catholics so closely that there is hardly any meaningful difference between them, except that Catholics unite faith to goodwill but Protestants separate the two. In fact, the agreement between them is so little known that even theology professors are going to be astounded by this statement.

The reason why this is unknown is that Roman Catholics rarely turn to God our Savior; they turn instead to the pope as Christ's vicar, and also to the saints. Therefore they have let their tenets regarding the assigning of Christ's merit and our being justified by faith lie dormant. Nevertheless, the points above in §§3, 4, 5, 6, 7, and 8 taken from the Council of Trent (which were ratified by Pope Pius IV, as shown in §2) make it abundantly clear that these are among the tenets that are received and acknowledged by Catholics. Compare these with the tenets from the Augsburg Confession and the *Formula of Concord* in §§9, 10, 11, and 12, and you can see that the distinctions between them are not substantial; they are merely verbal. By reading and carefully comparing the quotations earlier in this work, the church's theology professors will indeed be able to see (although not fully) the agreement between the Protestant and the Catholic views on these points. Some further illustrations of the agreement will be given in the following sections, so that theology professors, and also less highly educated clergy and lay people, will be able to see it.

3

The leading reformers—Luther, Melanchthon, and Calvin—retained **21** *all the dogmas regarding the trinity of persons in the Divine, original sin, the assigning of Christ's merit to us, and our being justified by faith, in the same past and present form they had had among Roman Catholics. The reformers separated goodwill or good works from that faith, however, and declared that our good works contribute nothing to our salvation, for the purpose of clearly differentiating themselves from Roman Catholics with regard to the essentials of the church, which are faith and goodwill.*

Brief Analysis

Books on ecclesiastical history make it clear that the four points just men- **22** tioned, as they are taught in the Protestant churches today, are not new. They were not invented by these three reformers. Instead, they had come into existence as early as the time of the Council of Nicaea and had been passed down by writers after that; they have been preserved as part of the tradition of the Roman Catholic Church.

The reason why Roman Catholics and Protestants agree concerning the trinity of persons in the Divine is that they both recognize the three [ecumenical] creeds in which this concept of a trinity is taught: the Apostles' Creed; the Nicene Creed; and the Athanasian Creed.

As for the notion that Christ's merit is assigned to us, the material gathered above in §§3–8 from the Council of Trent and in §§10–15 from the *Formula of Concord* makes it clear that they agree on this point as well.

As for the point about how we are justified, this will now be taken up for further discussion.

23 The Council of Trent has the following to say in regard to the faith that makes us just: The perpetual consent of the Catholic Church has been that faith is the beginning of human salvation, and the foundation and root of all justification. Without faith, it is impossible to please God and to come into the company of his children; see §5a above. The same document also says that faith comes from hearing the Word of God; see §§4d, [8].

As you can fully see from statements given above in §§4, 5, 7, and 8, that Roman Catholic council united faith and goodwill or faith and good works. The Protestant churches, named for the founders mentioned above, separated faith and goodwill or good works, however, and declared that the ingredient that actually saves us is faith and not goodwill or good works; they separated the two so as to differentiate themselves from Roman Catholics with regard to goodwill and faith, since these two are the essential characteristics of the church. I have heard this assertion a number of times from the founders of the Protestant churches themselves.

I have also heard from them that they reinforced this separation [of faith and goodwill] with arguments such as the following: On our own, none of us can do the type of good things that contribute to our salvation; we cannot fulfill the law either. They also separated faith and goodwill to prevent our own sense of merit (which arises from doing good works) from becoming part of our faith.

From the statements presented from the *Formula of Concord* in §12 above it is clear that the points just made were the origins and purposes behind the Protestant denial that good actions and goodwill play any role in our acquisition of faith and therefore of salvation. The following are among the statements presented there: Faith actually does not make us just if it has been formed through acts of goodwill, although Catholics say it does; see §12b. For many reasons we must reject the proposition that good works are necessary for our salvation. One reason is that Papists adopted these views in support of a bad cause; see §12h. People ought to reject the decree of the Council of Trent [and whatever else is used to support the opinion] that our good works preserve and maintain our salvation and faith; see §12m. Not to mention many other such statements in the *Formula of Concord.*

In the following sections [§§24–27] you will see that Protestants do in fact unite faith and goodwill and attribute to them a shared power to save; the only difference between the Protestant and the Roman Catholic views concerns how our good works come into existence.

4

The leaders of the Protestant Reformation do indeed describe good works as an appendage to faith and even an integral part of faith, but they say we are passive in the doing of them, whereas Roman Catholics say we are active in the doing of them. There is actually strong agreement between Protestants and Catholics on the subjects of faith, works, and our rewards. **24**

Brief Analysis

The books, sermons, and other sayings of the leaders of the Protestant Reformation make it clear that although those leaders separated faith and goodwill, nevertheless they did say that goodwill was an appendage to faith and eventually even an integral part of it. Nevertheless they tried to avoid bringing the two together and giving them a shared or concurrent power to save. After those leaders have stated that faith and goodwill are separate, they go on to unite them, and in fact express that union in clear and unambiguous wording. For example, they say that after we go through the process of being made just, our faith is never alone—our faith brings with it goodwill or good works, and if it does not, it is dead rather than living; see §13n, o, p, q, v, y. In fact, they state that good works necessarily follow faith; see §13u, v, w; and that the reborn use their new powers and gifts to cooperate with the Holy Spirit; see §13x. **25**

From the statements gathered above from the Council of Trent in §§4, 5, 6, 7, 8, it is clear that Roman Catholics present exactly the same teachings.

26 Protestants say almost exactly the same things as Roman Catholics do about the rewards we gain for our good works, as is clear from the statements copied from the *Formula of Concord* above to the effect that, because of the promises made to us and because of grace, our good works are deserving of both physical and spiritual rewards; see §14i, j, k, m; and that God crowns his gifts with rewards; see §14h, m.

Very similar statements occur in the Council of Trent, namely, that because of his grace, God makes his gifts our rewards; see §5f; and that salvation comes not as a result of our good works but as a result of God's promise and grace, because it is God who produces those good works through the Holy Spirit; see §5e, f, g, h, i, j.

27 At first glance, these pairs of statements make it appear as though there is complete agreement between Protestants and Catholics. Protestants, to prevent this from actually being the case, drew a distinction between *the works of the law,* which flow forth from our own will and are part of our own plan, and *the works of the Spirit,* which flow forth from faith as a free and spontaneous source; these good works they call the fruits of faith; see §§11h, k; 13a, i, k; 15k.

If you put the statements of both parties side by side and look deeply at them, you will observe that the two see no difference in the works themselves; all the difference lies in how the works come about. That is, Protestants see us as playing a *passive* role in the production of these good works, whereas Catholics see us as playing an *active* role in them. Therefore the Protestant view is that good works occur spontaneously as if they were coming from our intellect but not at the same time from our will. They say this because people cannot help being aware of good works when they are occurring, since the people themselves are doing them, and becoming aware is a function of the intellect.

Nevertheless, Protestants also preach that we are to practice repentance and to battle against [the desires of] our own flesh; see §13d, e, f, g, h, j. Since we cannot do these things without having a plan and exercising our own will—that is, acting seemingly as if we were doing so on our own—therefore the two positions agree in actuality.

28 Now, it might appear as though the two camps have opposite beliefs regarding whether we have free choice or not in our conversion or in the process by which we are made just. In fact, though, the two actually do agree with each other, as we can see if we consider in the right way the statements written in the Council of Trent; see §6a, b; and compare these with the things written in the *Formula of Concord;* see §15m. All the people in the Christian world have been baptized. Christians therefore have free choice, which allows them not only to hear the Word of God but also to agree with it and embrace it with faith. Therefore no one in Christianity is like a log of wood.

The points just presented illustrate the truths stated in §§19 and 21, **29** that Roman Catholics were the source the leading reformers drew on for their own teachings on the trinity of persons in the Divine, original sin, the assigning of Christ's merit to us, and our being justified by faith alone.

The purpose of these points has been to show the origin of these key Protestant teachings, especially how the separation of faith from good works and the teaching concerning faith alone came about. Protestants arrived at this for the sole purpose of differentiating themselves from Roman Catholics. Yet this disagreement was more a matter of semantics than of real substance.

The quotations given at the beginning of the book [§§9–15] clearly reveal the foundation on which the faith of the Protestant churches was built and what inspired the development of that faith.

5

The entire theology in the Christian world today is based on the idea **30** *that there are three gods—an idea that has arisen from the teaching that there is a trinity of persons.*

Brief Analysis

First I will say something about the origins of the idea that there is a trinity **31** of persons in the Divine, and therefore there are three gods. There are three creeds that specifically mention a trinity; they are known as the Apostles' Creed, the Nicene Creed, and the Athanasian Creed. The Apostles' Creed and the Nicene Creed mention the Trinity; the Athanasian Creed specifies a trinity of persons.

These three creeds are found in many psalm books. The Apostles' Creed is set to music in a hymn that is sung; the Nicene Creed appears after the Ten Commandments; and the Athanasian Creed appears by itself.

The Apostles' Creed was actually written after the time of the apostles. The Nicene Creed was written as part of the council that was held in the Bithynian city of Nicaea. In the year 325 the emperor Constantine summoned all the bishops of the Near East, Africa, and Europe to attend this council. After the council, some person or people composed the Athanasian Creed for the purpose of overthrowing the Arians; later on it was received by many churches as an ecumenical creed.

The first two creeds led to the confession of the Trinity. The third, the Athanasian Creed, promoted the claim that there was a trinity of persons; as we will see in the following sections [§§33–34], this led to the idea that there are three gods.

32 The existence of the divine Trinity is made very clear by the Lord's words in Matthew:

> Jesus said, "Go forth and make disciples of all the nations, baptizing them in the name of the Father, the Son, and the Holy Spirit." (Matthew 28:19)

The existence of the Trinity is also made clear by the following words in Matthew:

> When Jesus was being baptized, behold, the heavens were opened and he saw the Holy Spirit coming down like a dove upon him; and a voice from heaven said, "This is my beloved Son, in whom I am well pleased." (Matthew 3:16, 17)

The reason why the Lord sent his disciples forth to baptize people in the name of the Father, Son, and Holy Spirit was that this divine trinity existed within him in his then-glorified state. In the verse preceding the quotation from Matthew 28 just given, the Lord says, "All power has been given *to me* in heaven and on earth" (Matthew 28:18); and in the verse following, he says, "Behold *I* am with you all the days, even to the close of the age" (Matthew 28:20). In these verses, then, he mentions only himself and not three persons. In John we read, "There was not the Holy Spirit yet because Jesus was not yet glorified" (John 7:39). He made the statement in Matthew *after* he was glorified, and his glorification was when he became fully united with his Father, the divinity that had been inside him since conception. The Holy Spirit was the divine quality that emanated from him once he was glorified (John 20:22).

Why was the Athanasian Creed and its statements about a trinity of persons particularly responsible for leading to the idea of three gods? Because the word "person" leads to that idea, and also because the following words in that creed sow this notion: "The Father is one person, the Son another, and the Holy Spirit another." Also the statement a little further on: "The Father is God and Lord, the Son is God and Lord, and the Holy Spirit is God and Lord." The statement mainly responsible, however, is the following: "Just as Christian truth compels us to confess each person individually as God and Lord, so the catholic religion forbids us to say that there are three gods or three lords." The thrust of these words is that because of Christian truth we should confess and acknowledge three gods or lords, but because of the catholic religion we are not allowed to say or name three gods or lords. Therefore we should have the idea of three gods or lords but not confess them orally.

Nevertheless, the trinity as taught in the Athanasian Creed is in harmony with the truth, provided that in place of a trinity of *persons* you substitute a trinity in *one person*—the trinity that exists within God the Savior Jesus Christ (see *Teachings for the New Jerusalem on the Lord,* published in Amsterdam in 1763, §§55–61).

Consider the fact that the Apostles' Creed says "I believe in God, the Father," "in Jesus Christ," and "in the Holy Spirit"; and the Nicene Creed says "I believe in one God, the Father," "in one Lord, Jesus Christ," "and in the Holy Spirit." These are statements of belief in one God. The Athanasian Creed, however, speaks of God the Father, God the Son, and God the Holy Spirit; therefore this is a statement of belief in three gods.

Because the authors of and adherents to the Athanasian Creed saw very clearly that the statements it makes would lead inevitably to the idea of three gods, they aimed to remedy this problem by saying that the three share the same substance and essence. All that this accomplished, however, was to make people think that the three gods agree and share the same point of view. Attributing one undivided substance and essence to three things does not eliminate the idea that there are three things.

It merely introduces confusion, because "substance" and "essence" are metaphysical terms, and for all the power that metaphysics possesses, it cannot make one entity out of three persons, each of whom is God. It can lead people to speak of three as one, but it can never make them think of three as one.

35 As for the assertion made above [§30] that the entire theology in the Christian world today is based on the idea that there are three gods, clear evidence for this comes from the Christian teaching regarding justification, which is the primary teaching of the church among Christians both Roman Catholic and Protestant.

The teaching on justification states that God the Father sent his Son to redeem and save human beings. God the Father also gives the Holy Spirit to carry out this work.

All people who hear, read, or say this cannot avoid dividing God into three in their thinking, that is, in the mental image they have. They cannot avoid the sense that one god sent another and works through a third.

As I will demonstrate later on in other parts of this text [§§40, 54, 61, 64–69], the thought that the divine Trinity is divided into three persons, each of whom is God, permeates all the other teachings of the church of today, as what comes from the head permeates the entire body.

Meanwhile, I invite you to look at the quotations on justification at the beginning of the book [§§2–15], and consider points of Christian theology both generally and in detail. Also look within yourself when you hear preaching in church or prayers at home: Are you picturing or thinking of anything other than three gods? Pay particular attention to the times when you are praying or singing to one of the three by himself or to the other two by themselves, as frequently happens.

These considerations support the truth of the proposition that the entire theology in the Christian world today is based on the idea that there are three gods.

36 The concept of a trinity of gods goes against Sacred Scripture, as we all know. We read,

> Am not I Jehovah? And there is no God other than me. I am a just God, and there is no Savior other than me. (Isaiah 45:21–22)

> I am Jehovah your God. You are to acknowledge no God other than me. There is no Savior other than me. (Hosea 13:4)

Thus says Jehovah the King of Israel, and Israel's Redeemer, Jehovah Sabaoth: "I am the First and the Last, and there is no God other than me." (Isaiah 44:6)

Jehovah Sabaoth is his name, and your Redeemer, the Holy One of Israel. He will be called the God of the whole earth. (Isaiah 54:5)

On that day Jehovah will become king over all the earth. On that day Jehovah will be one, and his name one. (Zechariah 14:9)

There are many more passages like this elsewhere in the Word as well.

The concept of a trinity of gods also goes against enlightened reason, as many arguments are capable of establishing. What person of sound reason would be open to hearing that three gods created the world? Or that creating and preserving, redeeming and saving, and reforming and regenerating are tasks undertaken by three gods, not one God? On the other hand, what person of sound reason would *not* be open to hearing that the same God who created us also redeems, regenerates, and saves us? Since the latter thoughts are reasonable, but the former are not, every group of religious and reasonable people on the face of this earth acknowledges that there is one God. **37**

As we all know, Muslims and some of the peoples in Asia and Africa detest Christianity because they believe it entails the worship of three gods. When Christians are rebuked on this account, they have only one response: that the three persons share one essence, and therefore constitute one God.

I can attest that the reasoning power granted me allows me to see that no world, no angelic heaven, no church, and nothing within any of them could have come into existence or could continue to exist if there were not one God.

I would like to add to this a few sentences from the Belgic Confession, which was officially adopted at the Synod of Dort: **38**

I believe in one God, who is one single essence, in whom there are three persons, really, truly, and eternally distinct according to their incommunicable properties—namely, Father, Son, and Holy Spirit. The Father is the cause, origin, and source of all things, visible as well as invisible. The Son is the Word, the wisdom, and the image of the Father. The Holy Spirit is the eternal power and might, proceeding from the Father and the Son. But it must be said that this teaching far surpasses human understanding; we are waiting to know it fully in heaven. (Belgic Confession [8, 9])

6

39 *Once we reject the idea of a trinity of persons and therefore the idea that there are three gods, and accept in its place that there is one God and that the divine trinity exists within him, we see how wrong the teachings of today's Christian theology are.*

Brief Analysis

40 The teachings of today's Christian theology are based on an idea of three gods, an idea that resulted from taking the teaching that there is a trinity of persons at face value. We see the wrongness of those teachings only *after* we have accepted in their place the idea that there is one God and that the divine trinity exists within him, because seeing how wrong those teachings are is not possible *before* making that switch.

Before that, we are like people at night who are looking at various objects in the light of only a few stars; we see statues and mistake them for living human beings. Or we are like people lying in bed in the twilight before dawn, seeing something like ghosts in the air above them and thinking the apparitions are angels. Or we are like people who see any number of things in the dim, deceptive light of their own imagination and believe them to be real. It is well known that the true nature of things like that is not detected and does not become apparent until we come into the light of day—that is, the light of intellectual wakefulness. When genuine truths come forth to be seen in their own light, which is the light of heaven, the same thing happens to teachings of the church that have been mistakenly or falsely understood and reinforced.

Surely everyone is capable of understanding that all teachings based on the idea of three gods are inwardly wrong and false. I say "inwardly" because the idea of God is central to everything having to do with the church, religious practice, and worship. Theological concepts dwell at a higher level in the human mind than all other concepts, and the highest theological concept is the idea of God. Therefore if our idea of God is false, everything else that follows from it derives a falseness from or becomes falsified by the source from which it originates. Whatever is highest (which is also what is inmost) acts as the essence of the things that result from it lower down. That essence, like a soul, forms those lower things into a kind of body that is an image of itself. If that essence is false, and it descends and encounters truths lower down, it taints them with its own blight and error.

Our having the idea of three gods in our theological concepts can be compared to patients' having a disease that persists in their hearts or lungs, but the patients consider themselves healthy because their doctor, unaware of their underlying condition, has convinced them they are well. A doctor who knows about their disease, however, and still convinces them they are well deserves to be and should be charged with causing immeasurable harm.

7

After we make this change, the faith we then acknowledge and accept 41 *is a faith that is truly effective for our salvation—a faith in one God, united to good works.*

Brief Analysis

When our former faith (a faith in three gods) disappears, then we acknowl- 42 edge and accept this faith (a faith in one God) as a faith that is truly able to save us. The reason for this is that the face of faith in one God was not previously visible to us. Preachers claim that the modern-day faith is the only faith that can save us, because it is a faith in one God and because it is a faith in the Savior. Yet that faith is two-faced. One face is internal; the other is external. The internal face of that faith takes the form of pictur-ing that there are three gods. (Who has a different picture or thought than this? All should examine themselves and see.) The external face of that faith, however, takes the form of confessing one God. (Who con-fesses or speaks of anything other than this? All should examine them-selves and see.)

These two faces disagree with each other so completely that the external face is not acknowledged by the internal face and the inter-nal face is not recognized by the external face. This disagreement and this disappearance of the one from the sight of the other has generated mental confusion on the part of the church regarding the means of being saved.

Something very different occurs, however, when the internal face and the external face are in agreement, recognize each other, and see each other as being of the same mind. As should be intrinsically obvious, this takes place when we not only see with our mind's eye but also acknowledge with our mouth that there is one God and that the divine trinity exists within him.

Once we accept this faith, any notion that the Father was at one time alienated from the human race and was later reconciled to it is completely abolished. Instead there comes forth an entirely new view of the assignment of credit or blame, the forgiving of sins, and the process of being regenerated and therefore being saved. In the work itself, all this will become very clear in a rational light made brighter by divine truths from Sacred Scripture.

The reason why the proposition says that this faith is united to good works is that it is not even possible to have faith in the one God if that faith is not united to good works.

8

43 *This faith is faith in God the Savior Jesus Christ. In a simple form it is this: (1) There is one God, the divine trinity exists within him, and he is the Lord Jesus Christ. (2) Believing in him is a faith that saves. (3) We must abstain from doing things that are evil—they belong to the Devil and come from the Devil. (4) We must do things that are good—they belong to God and come from God. (5) We must do these things as if we ourselves were doing them, but we must believe that they come from the Lord working with us and through us.*

Brief Analysis

44 The proposition just stated is the faith of the new church in a simple form. This faith can be seen in fuller detail in the appendix to this volume [§§116–117], and in complete detail in the first part of the work itself. That first part will present teachings concerning the Lord God the Savior and the trinity that exists within him; about love for God and love for our neighbor; and about faith and its partnership with these two loves. This faith will also be covered point by point in the rest of the work. Here, however, it is important to present at least a few items of support to illustrate this preliminary statement of the faith.

The following are a few arguments and passages to support the *first point* in the proposition—that there is one God, that the divine trinity exists within him, and that he is the Lord Jesus Christ.

It is a fixed and constant truth that there is one God, that his essence is indivisible, and that there is a trinity. Given that there is one God and that his essence is indivisible, it follows that God is one person. And since he is one person, it follows that the trinity exists within that one person.

It is clear that the Lord Jesus Christ is God; he was conceived by God the Father (Luke 1:34, 35), and therefore God is the soul and the life within him. As he himself has said, the Father and he are one (John 10:30); he is in the Father and the Father is in him (John 14:10, 11); anyone who sees and knows him sees and knows the Father (John 14:7, 9); no one sees or knows the Father except the one who is close to the Father's heart (John 1:18); all things that the Father has are his (John 3:35; 16:15); and he is the way, the truth, and the life, and no one comes to the Father except through him (John 14:6). (So we come to the Father by him because the Father is in him and is him.)

Paul says that all the fullness of divinity dwells physically in Jesus Christ (Colossians 2:9). Isaiah says, "A Child has been born to us; a Son has been given to us. His name will be called God, *Father of Eternity*" (Isaiah 9:6). Furthermore, he has power over all flesh (John 17:2) and has all power in heaven and on earth (Matthew 28:18). From these quotations it is clear that he is the God of heaven and earth.

The *second point* in the proposition—that believing in him is a faith that saves—is supported by the following passages.

Jesus said, "Anyone who believes in me will live and will never die." (John 11:25, 26)

This is the will of the Father, that all those who believe in the Son will have eternal life. (John 6:40)

God loved the world so much that he gave his only-begotten Son so that everyone who believes in him would not perish but would have eternal life. (John 3:15, 16)

Those who believe in the Son have eternal life. Those who do not believe in the Son will not see life; instead, the wrath of God abides on them. (John 3:36)

As for the *remaining three points* in the proposition—that we must abstain from doing things that are evil because they belong to the Devil and come from the Devil; we must do things that are good because they belong to God and come from God; but we must believe that this abstaining and doing come from the Lord working with us and through us—there is no need to illustrate or demonstrate these points. The entirety of Sacred Scripture from beginning to end supports them. Briefly put, the Word teaches nothing else but that we should abstain from things that are evil, do things that are good, and believe in the Lord God.

There is no such thing as a religious practice that lacks these three elements. Religious practice has to do with life; life is abstaining from things that are evil and doing things that are good; and none of us can abstain from evil or do good without the help of the Lord. Therefore if you remove these three from the church, you are removing both Sacred Scripture and religious practice from the church, and once these are removed, the church is no longer a church.

For the faith of the new church in a universal form and a specific form, see §§116, 117 below.

All these points will be demonstrated in the work itself.

9

45 *The faith of today has removed living a religious life from the church. A religious life consists in acknowledging one God and worshiping him with a faith that is connected to goodwill.*

Brief Analysis

46 Surely every group of religious and reasonable people on the face of the earth knows and believes that there is one God; that doing good things is being with God; that doing evil things goes against God; that we must apply our own soul, heart, and powers to doing what is good and not doing what is evil, even though these faculties and abilities actually flow into us from God; and that the religious life consists in doing all the above. Surely everyone can see, then, that to confess three persons within the Divine and to declare that salvation has nothing to do with good works is to remove religious life from the church.

The Protestant assertion that salvation has nothing to do with good works is made in the following passages. Faith makes us just apart from good works; see §12a, b. Good works are not necessary either for our salvation or for our faith, because salvation and faith are not preserved or maintained by our good works; see §12g, h, l, m. Therefore there is no bond that unites faith and good works.

If we go back to the assertion that good works nevertheless spontaneously follow faith like fruit issuing forth from a tree—see §13k, m— then we must ask this: Who does these good works? In fact, who would bother thinking about them or feel spontaneously moved to do them when they know and believe that these works contribute nothing to their salvation, and that none of us on our own can do any good for our own salvation, and so on?

If someone asserts that Protestants do nonetheless unite good works to their faith, I reply that if you deeply examine that union, you find that it is not actually a uniting but rather an appending of good works to faith. Good works are an appendage that is tacked on; they are not an integral part or even securely attached. They are like the shadows that are added to a painting to make it look more realistic. Religious practice, though, has to do with our lives; it consists in good works that we do in accordance with the truths taught by our faith. Clearly, then, religious practice is not in actuality an appendage; it is the thing itself.

To many people, though, living a religious life is like a horse's tail; you can remove it if you want, because it serves no purpose. Who could come to any other reasonable conclusion from statements such as the following when taken at face value?

> It is foolish to dream that the works enjoined by the second tablet of the Ten Commandments make us just before God; see §12d.

> Any who believe they will gain salvation because they do acts of goodwill are insulting Christ; see §12e.

> Good works must be completely excluded from any discussion of our justification and eternal life; see §12f.

There are many other such statements there as well.

When we go on to read that good works necessarily follow faith, and that if they do not follow faith, our faith is false and not true (see §130, p, v, and many other passages), who among us pays any attention to this? Or if we do pay attention to it, do we do good works *consciously?* Because good works that somehow flow out of us when we are unaware of them are surely as lifeless as if they had been done by a statue.

If we look more deeply into the cause of this teaching, we find that the leading reformers first assumed faith alone as their standard dogma in order to be differentiated from Roman Catholics, as I mentioned above (§§21, 22, 23). Later on they attached acts of goodwill so as not to go against Sacred Scripture and so that their denomination would be viewed as a religion and something wholesome.

10

47 *The faith taught by the modern-day church is incapable of being united to acts of goodwill; it is incapable of producing any fruit in the form of good works.*

Brief Analysis

48 Before I demonstrate this proposition, I will first lay before the intellect what goodwill is and where it comes from, what faith is and where it comes from, and therefore what the good works called "fruits" are and where they come from.

Faith is truth. Therefore teachings of faith are the same as teachings of truth. Teachings of truth affect our intellect, and therefore how we think, and what we say as a result. They teach us what we should will and what we should do. They teach that some things are evil and we should abstain from them; they teach that some things are good and we should do them. When we follow these teachings and actually do what is good, our good actions enter into a partnership with the truths we understand, because in these actions our will works together with our intellect. (Good actions have to do with our will and truth has to do with our intellect.) This partnership leads us to a love for what is good, which is the essence of goodwill, and a love for what is true, which is the essence of faith. When combined, these two form a marriage. Good works are the offspring born of this marriage, just as pieces of fruit are the offspring produced by a tree. As a result, there are fruits that are born of goodness and fruits that are born of truth. In the Word, the latter are represented as grapes and the former as olives.

Once we accept that this is the origin of good works, it becomes clear that faith alone can never produce or give birth to any of the works that are known as fruits, any more than a woman by herself without a man can produce any offspring. Therefore "the fruits of faith" is a made-up, meaningless expression.

Nothing in the whole universe was or is ever produced unless it comes from a marriage of two things, one of which relates to goodness and the other to truth, or else one of which relates to evil and the other to falsity. Therefore no works could even be conceived, let alone born, if these two elements did not enter into a kind of marriage. Good actions are produced by a marriage of goodness and truth; evil actions are produced by a marriage of evil and falsity.

Goodwill cannot be united to the faith of the modern-day church; there is no marriage there that could give birth to a good work. This is because the assigning of Christ's merit is thought to do everything for us. It is thought to forgive our crimes, to make us just, to regenerate us, to sanctify us, and to give us salvation and the life of heaven—and all for free with no effort on our part. If this is true, though, what is goodwill and what is its supposed marriage with faith? It is pointless and meaningless. What is goodwill but an accessory or an adjunct to the assigning of Christ's merit and to the process whereby we are made just? Goodwill is good for nothing.

Furthermore, a faith based on the idea that there are three gods is wrong, as I have shown above (see §§39, 40). How can true goodwill have a relationship with a wrongheaded faith?

There are two reasons people give for believing that the modern-day faith has no bond with goodwill. One is that they describe this faith as spiritual in nature, but they see goodwill as merely earthly and moral in nature; and in their opinion no relationship is possible between what is spiritual and what is earthly. The second reason they give is to keep anything that comes from ourselves, and therefore any desire for reward, from becoming mixed up with our faith, since faith is the only thing that saves us.

It is in fact true that there is no bond between goodwill and *that* faith; but there is a bond between goodwill and the *new* faith, as described in §§116, 117.

II

51 *The faith of the modern-day church results in worship that engages our mouths but not our lives. How acceptable the Lord finds the worship of our mouths, though, depends on how worshipful our lives are.*

Brief Analysis

52 Experience supports this point. How many people today live by the Ten Commandments and the Lord's other precepts as a religious practice? How many people today are willing to look their own evils in the face and practice actual repentance, thereby initiating a worshipful life? How many devout people practice a repentance that is more than merely verbal and theatrical—confessing that they are sinners and praying (in obedience to the teachings of the church) that God the Father have mercy for the sake of his Son, who suffered on the cross for their sins, took away the damning effect of those sins, and ritually purged them with his own blood? "May the Son forgive our crimes so that we may be presented spotless before the throne of your judgment."

Surely everyone can see that this kind of worship is not from the heart; it is only from the lungs. It is external but not internal. We are praying that our sins may be forgiven, yet we are unaware of a single sin within ourselves; and if we are aware of any sin, we either give it our favor and indulgence or else believe that we are purified and absolved of it by our faith without having to do any work of our own.

By way of comparison, this is like a servant coming in with his face and clothes covered in soot and dung, approaching his master, and saying, "Lord, wash me." Surely his master would tell him, "You foolish servant! What are you saying? Look, there is the water, the soap, and a towel. Don't you have hands? Don't they work? Wash yourself!"

The Lord God is going to say, "The means of being purified come from me. Your willingness and your power come from me. Therefore use these gifts and endowments of mine as your own and you will be purified."

Allow me to mention another example. If you prayed a thousand times both at home and in church for God the Father to protect you for his Son's sake from the Devil, yet you yourself did not use the freedom the Lord was constantly providing you with to protect yourself from evil or the Devil, you could not be kept safe even by legions of angels sent especially to you by the Lord.

The Lord cannot act contrary to his own divine design. His design is for us to examine ourselves, see our evils, and resist them; and to do this seemingly on our own, although in fact the Lord is helping. Nowadays this does not seem like the gospel, but it is—being saved by the Lord is the gospel.

As for why the worship of our mouths is only acceptable to the Lord depending on how worshipful our lives are: Before God and before angels the sound of our speech reflects how much we long for love and faith; and it is the way we live that determines whether love and faith are present in us or not. If love and faith in God are present in your life, to God and the angels you sound like a dove. If love for yourself and confidence in yourself are present in your life, you sound like a screech owl, no matter how you twist your voice around to mimic the sound of a turtledove. The spiritual quality present within the sound produces this effect.

12

The body of teaching espoused by the modern-day church is woven together out of numerous absurdities that have to be taken on faith. Therefore its teachings become part of our memory alone. They do not become part of our higher understanding; they rest instead on supporting evidence from below the level of the intellect. **53**

Brief Analysis

The leaders of the church today insist that the intellect has to be held under obedience to faith. In fact, they say that true faith is a faith in the unknown— a blind faith, a faith of the night. **54**

This is the first absurdity. Faith has to do with truth and truth has to do with faith. In order for truth to become part of our faith, we have to see it in its own light; otherwise what we are believing in could be false.

There are many further absurdities that flow forth from faith as the church today defines it: God the Father bore a Son from eternity. The Holy Spirit emanates from both the Father and the Son. Each of these three is a person and a god in his own right. Both the body and the soul of the Lord originated from his mother. These three persons, and therefore three gods, created the universe. One of them came down and took on a human manifestation in order to reconcile the Father to us and save us. We are saved through the assigning, attributing, and transferring of his justice to those of us who by grace have acquired faith and believe the absurdities just listed. Prior to receiving that faith, we are like a statue, a log of wood, or a stone. Just hearing the Word allows faith to flow into us. Faith alone has the power to save us apart from the works of the law, even if that faith is untouched by goodwill. Faith produces a forgiveness of our sins without our having to go through repentance first. On the basis of that forgiveness of sins and nothing else, even if we have not repented we are nevertheless made just, regenerated, and sanctified. Then goodwill, good works, and a restoration of wisdom spontaneously come upon us.

From the body of teaching based on the idea of three gods, these and many other teachings like them flow forth like illegitimate offspring conceived as the result of an ongoing illicit affair.

55 Surely anyone with any wisdom can see that ideas like these only become part of our memory; they do not become part of our higher understanding, even though they can be supported by reasoning based on appearances and mistaken impressions from below the intellect.

There are two kinds of light that shine in the human intellect: one from heaven, and the other from the world. The light from heaven, which is spiritual in nature, flows into human minds at a level above the memory. Light from the world, which is earthly in nature, flows in at a level below the memory. As I have shown in the *memorable occurrence* that appears in §233 of my recently published work *Marriage Love,* in light from the world we can support whatever concepts we like. False concepts are as easy to support as true ones; and after we have given them support, we see false ideas as completely true.

To this I will add the following secret from heaven. Depending on **56** how much support and reinforcement we have given the absurd teachings mentioned above, they all stay together in our minds as if they were woven into a single bundle or glued to form one big lump. They all at the same time become part of any individual pronouncement of a teaching of the church. For example, when "faith" is mentioned, or "goodwill," or "repentance," and even more so if "the assigning of Christ's merit" is mentioned, or "the process of being made just," all the other teachings are present as well. The person making the statement does not see that heap or conglomeration of ideas, but the angels who are with the person do see it. They call it *malua,* that is, confusion and darkness.

I foresee that many people who are now steeped in the absurdities of **57** this faith are going to say, "How can the intellect grasp theological teachings at all? Isn't something spiritual a thing that is by definition transcendent? Go ahead, though, and see if you can open up the mysteries of redemption and justification so that human reason may see them and finally satisfy its curiosity!"

Anticipating this challenge, I will indeed open up these mysteries, as follows.

As everyone surely knows, there is one God; there is no God other than him. God is love itself and wisdom itself, or goodness itself and truth itself. God himself came down in the form of divine truth, which is the Word, and took on a human manifestation for the purpose of removing the hells, and therefore damnation, from the human race. He accomplished this through battles with and victories over the Devil, that is, over all the hells that were then attacking and trying to spiritually kill every person who came into the world. Afterward he glorified his human manifestation; he did this by uniting divine truth to divine goodness within himself. In this way he returned to the Father from whom he had come forth.

Once we realize this, we understand the following statement in John: "The Word was with God, and the Word was God. And the Word became flesh" (John 1:1, 14). And in the same Gospel, "I came forth from the Father and have come into the world. Again, I leave the world and go to the Father" (John 16:28). From the points just made it should also be clear that if the Lord had not come into the world, no one could have been saved, and that the people who are saved are the people who believe in him and live good lives.

This is the face of faith. It appears before our [inner] sight when we have allowed the Word to bring us into the light of day. It is the face of the faith of the new church. (See *the faith of the new heaven and the new church in universal form and in a specific form* below, §§116, 117.)

13

58 *The tenets of the church of today are extremely difficult to learn and retain. They cannot be preached or taught without a great deal of restraint and caution to keep them from appearing in their naked state, since true reason would not recognize or accept them.*

Brief Analysis

59 The statement that the intellect has to be held under obedience to faith serves as a kind of standard opening disclaimer for the tenets of the church of today. (See §54 above for an indication that what lies within them are mysteries or secrets so "transcendent" that they are incapable of flowing into the higher regions of the intellect and making sense.)

When still in school, ambitious ministers in the church who long to have a reputation as outstandingly wise and to be considered oracles in spiritual matters give special attention to teachings that are beyond the grasp of others. Although these teachings are very difficult for them to learn, they pursue them avidly. When, as a result, they gain a reputation for being wise, and become rich and famous because they possess these hidden treasures, they are granted the caps of distinguished professors or the robes of bishops.

In their thinking and in their teaching from the pulpit they focus almost exclusively on the mysteries concerning justification by faith alone and the good works that serve as faith's lowly servants. Drawing on all they know about faith and good works, they have an amazing way of separating the two at one moment and bringing them together at another.

It is as if they were holding naked faith in one hand and works of goodwill in the other. At one moment they extend their arms wide to separate them; at another, they bring their hands together and combine the two.

Let some examples serve as illustrations. They teach that good works are not necessary for our salvation, because if we ourselves are doing them, we are doing them for some reward. Yet at the same time, they teach that good works do necessarily follow the faith that, for them, is the same as salvation itself.

They teach that faith without good works is alive and justifies us. Yet at the same time they teach that faith without good works is dead and does not justify us.

They teach that faith is not preserved or maintained by good works. Yet at the same time they teach that good works flow forth from faith like fruit from a tree, light from the sun, and heat from a fire.

They teach that good works, when *appended* to faith, bring it to fulfillment. Yet at the same time they teach that when good works are *united* as in a marriage or constitute a single form, they deprive faith of its essential ability to save us.

They teach that Christians are not under the law, and yet at the same time they teach that Christians must have a daily practice of following the law.

They teach that our good works are harmful if they become entangled in our being saved by faith—for example, if they become involved in our being forgiven our sins, justified, regenerated, brought to life, or saved. Yet they teach that our good works are profitable to us as long as they do not become entangled in our faith.

They teach that God gives us good works and crowns them with rewards, including spiritual rewards, but not with salvation or eternal life, because these are the rewards with which he crowns a faith that is separate from good works.

They teach that this faith of theirs is like a queen, who parades in magnificence because she is attended by good works as servants following along behind; but if these good works embrace her face-to-face and give her a kiss, she will be dethroned and called a whore.

Especially when they teach about the interaction between faith and good works, they suggest that from one point of view the interaction is beneficial and from another point of view it is not. They carefully choose particular words and skillfully weave them together in such a way that what they say has two meanings. There is one meaning for lay people and another for clergy. The meaning aimed at lay people covers up what they are really saying, but the meaning aimed at clergy reveals it.

Consider, if you will, whether any of the people who hear messages like these will be able to extract any teaching that will lead them to salvation? Will they not instead be blinded by the apparent contradictions in what is taught? And once blinded, will they not grope around for the means of salvation as if they were walking in total darkness? Based on the evidence of our own actions, which of us can tell whether we have any faith or not? Who knows whether it is better for us to do good works, because we fear missing out on the reward if we do not; or not to do good works, because we fear losing our faith if we do?

My friend, disentangle yourself from teachings like these. Abstain from what is evil because it is sinful, do what is good, and believe in the Lord. If you do these things, you will experience a process of being justified that will actually save you.

14

60 *The teachings of faith of the modern-day church attribute to God qualities that are merely human: they say, for example, that God looked at the human race with anger; that he needed to be reconciled to us; that he was in fact reconciled through his love for his Son and through the Son's intercession; that he needed to be appeased by seeing his Son's wretched suffering, and this brought him back into a merciful attitude; that he assigns the Son's justice to unjust people who beg him for it on the basis of their faith alone, and turns them from enemies into friends and from children of wrath into children of grace.*

Brief Analysis

61 Surely everyone knows that God is compassion and mercy itself. He is absolute love and absolute goodness. These qualities constitute his underlying reality or essence. Surely, then, everyone sees the contradiction in saying that compassion itself or absolute goodness could look at the human race with anger, become our enemy, turn away from us, and lock us all into damnation and nevertheless continue to be his own divine essence, to be God. Attitudes and actions of that kind belong to a wicked person, not a virtuous one. They belong to an angel of hell, not an angel of heaven. It is horrendous to attribute them to God.

The fact that things like this have been taught is clear from direct statements made by many of the founders, the councils, and the churches as a whole, from the first centuries of Christianity right up to the present day.

It is also clear from indirect evidence. There are derivative teachings that must have come from thoughts like these as their source, the way effects come from a cause or bodily actions from a brain. For instance, the notion that God needed to be reconciled to us; that he was in fact reconciled through his love for his Son and through the Son's intercession and mediation; that God needed to be appeased by seeing his Son's final wretched suffering, and that this brought him back and more or less forced him to adopt a merciful attitude; that God went from being our enemy to being our friend and adopted us (children of wrath that we are) as children of grace.

(For the point that it would be merely human behavior for God to assign the justice and rewards of his Son to unjust people who begged him for it on the basis on their faith alone, see the last analytical section in this little work [§112].)

There were theologians who assigned to God attributes that are merely human and unworthy of God. Their purpose in doing so was to preserve the integrity of the doctrine of justification, once it was established, and dress it up in some plausible fashion. They said that anger, revenge, damnation, and other things of the kind were traits possessed by God's justice, and this is why such things are mentioned so many times in the Word and are (seemingly) attributed to God. **62**

Mention of "the anger of God" in the Word actually refers to that which is evil in us. Because this evil goes against God it is called the anger of God. This expression does not mean that God is angry at us but that our own evil makes us angry at God. Because evil carries its own punishment with it (just as goodness carries its own reward), when evil brings punishment on us it looks as though God is punishing us.

This is the same, though, as criminals blaming the law for their own punishment, or our blaming the fire for burning us when we put our hand in it, or our blaming the drawn sword in the guard's hand when we hurl ourselves onto the tip of it. This is the nature of God's justice. (For more on these points, see *Revelation Unveiled.* On the justice and judgment that exist in God and come from God, see §668 there; on the Word attributing anger to God, see §§635, 658; on the Word attributing revenge to God, see §806.)

These are features of the Word's *literal* meaning. They occur because the literal meaning is written in correspondences and in expressions of an appearance. These features do not appear in the Word's *spiritual* meaning, however; in this meaning the truth stands forth in its own light.

I can attest that when angels hear anyone saying God was angry and locked the whole human race into damnation, or was reconciled from being our enemy through the Son as a second God born from the first God, they become like people who are about to vomit because their stomachs and internal organs have been violently heaved this way and that. The angels say, "What more insane thing could anyone possibly say about God?"

63   How did it come about that theologians attributed merely human qualities to God? The underlying cause is that all spiritual perception and enlightenment come from the Lord alone. The Lord is the Word, or divine truth. He is the true light that enlightens everyone (John 1:1, 9). He says, "I have come into the world as a light so that anyone who believes in me will not remain in darkness" (John 12:46). This light and the awareness that is gained from it flow only into people who acknowledge the Lord as the God of heaven and earth and who turn to him alone. This light and awareness do not flow into people who think in terms of three gods, as has been happening since the early establishment of the Christian church. Because the idea of three gods is an earthly notion, the only light it receives is earthly. It is incapable of opening up to receive any inflow of spiritual light. This is why the only qualities people have seen in God have been earthly in nature.

For another thing, if theologians had realized the vast incongruity between their ideas and the true divine essence, and had removed these ideas from the teachings on justification, this would obviously have amounted to a complete abandonment of a Christianity that had always been centered on the worship of three gods. [No alternative was available] before the predetermined time for the new church, when fullness and restoration would come.

15

64   *The faith of the modern-day church has given birth to horrifying off-spring in the past, and is producing more such offspring now: for example, the notion that there is instantaneous salvation as a result of the direct intervention of mercy; that there is predestination; that God cares only for our faith and pays no attention to our actions; that there is no bond that unites goodwill and faith; that as we undergo conversion we* *are like a log of wood; and many more teachings of the kind. Another problem has been the adoption of [false] principles of reason that are based on the teaching that we are justified by our faith alone and the teaching concerning the person of Christ, and the use of these principles to judge the uses and benefits of the sacraments (baptism and the Holy Supper). From the earliest centuries of Christianity until now, heresies have been leaping forth from a single source: the body of teaching based on the idea that there are three gods.*

Brief Analysis

The only kind of salvation people believe in today is an instantaneous salvation as a result of direct mercy. They say that a verbal statement of faith alone and a confidence expressed by the lungs takes care of everything we need in the way of salvation. There is no need for goodwill (even though in actuality goodwill is what allows verbal faith to become real faith, and allows confidence expressed by the lungs to become confidence felt at heart). If you remove the idea of a cooperation that we undertake seemingly on our own through our exercise of goodwill, then this cooperation that spontaneously and automatically follows faith becomes "a passive activity," which is a meaningless expression. What more, then, would we need than the following brief, direct statement: "Save me, O God, for the sake of the suffering of your Son. He washed away my sins with his own blood and is bringing me as a pure, just, and holy person before your throne"? If we had not made a statement like this before, even in our final hour before dying it would serve to initiate our justification. **65**

Section 340 in the work *Divine Providence,* published in Amsterdam in 1764, shows, however, that the concept of instantaneous salvation by direct mercy is the flying fiery serpent in the church today, that it is destroying the religion, that it gives people an unwarranted feeling of security, and that it blames God for our damnation.

Why does the proposition above describe predestination as an *offspring* of the faith of the modern-day church? Because this notion is born out of the belief that salvation is instantaneous by direct mercy, and also out of the belief that we are completely powerless and have no free choice in spiritual matters (see §69 below). **66**

As for the assertion that predestination follows the other concepts just mentioned like one fiery serpent after another or one spider after another, see above [§54]. We are also told that our conversion is lifeless, and in it we are like logs of wood; and once we are converted we have no awareness of whether or not the logs that we are have been brought to life yet by grace. For instance, we read that God produces faith where and when he wills in those who hear the Word; see §11a; that is, this is entirely up to him. Also that we gain the status of being the "elect" as a matter of pure grace on God's part exclusive of any action on our part, whether that action is initiated by the powers of our nature or of our reason (*Formula of Concord*, page 821; appendix, page 182). Even if we reflect upon them, the works that follow from our faith and testify to its existence look to us just like works of the flesh. The [Holy] Spirit that produces them does not reveal their origin; as with faith, he produces these works as a result of his grace and at his good pleasure.

[2] From these teachings it is clear that the dogma of predestination has arisen from the faith of today's church as a shoot arises from a root. I can assert that it flows forth as a scarcely avoidable by-product of that faith. A flowing forth like this first occurred among the Predestinarians; then another came from Gottschalk, and later on yet another from Calvin and his followers. Eventually the concept was firmly established by the Synod of Dort. From there it was imported by the Supralapsarians and the Infralapsarians as a sacred central effigy in their religion, or better yet, as the head of Medusa the Gorgon carved into the shield of Pallas [Athena herself].

[3] How could we attribute more harmfulness or cruelty to God than by believing that he predestines some members of the human race to hell? It would be believing in divine cruelty to think that the Lord, who is love itself and mercy itself, would want a multitude of people to be born for hell or millions to be born under a curse, that is, to be born devils and satans. It would be believing in divine cruelty to think that even though the Lord had divine wisdom, which is infinite, he would neglect to ensure through providence and foresight that those who live good lives and acknowledge God are not thrown into eternal fire and torment.

The Lord is in fact the Creator and Savior of all. He alone leads all people. He wishes the death of no one. It would be attributing great savagery to him to think and believe that the vast arrays of nations and populations under his divine guidance and watchful eye would just be handed over by predestination as prey to satiate the Devil's gaping jaws. This is the off-spring of the faith of today's church; the belief of the new church, though, abhors it as something monstrous.

The idea that God cares only for our faith and pays no attention to our actions is a new heresy concocted from the first two heresies, [instan-taneous salvation and predestination,] discussed just above in §§65, 66. It is amazing to note that when the wisest people of our age deeply exam-ined and unfolded the concepts within faith alone, they brought forth this idea as the third pup born of the she-wolf of predestination. Yet because this offspring is insane, ungodly, and Machiavellian, the pup is kept still wrapped up in its afterbirth to keep its hideousness out of sight. Its insanity and ungodliness is in fact described and rejected, though, in *Revelation Unveiled* 463. **67**

As for evidence that the modern-day church believes there is no bond uniting goodwill and faith, this is found in the following state-ments from its teachings regarding justification: Faith is attributed to us as righteousness apart from the works we do; see §12a. Faith actually does not make us just if it has been formed through acts of goodwill; see §12b. Good works must be completely excluded from any discussion of our justification and eternal life; see §12f. Good works are not necessary for our salvation; any assertion that they are necessary should be clearly rejected by the church; see §12g, h, i, j. Our salvation and our faith are not preserved or maintained by goodwill or its works; see §12l, m. Good works that are mixed up in the business of our being justified are harmful; see §14g. The works of the spirit or of grace that follow faith as its fruits contribute nothing to our salvation; see §14d and elsewhere [§§11b, 13w]. **68**

The inescapable conclusion from all these points is there is no bond between goodwill and that kind of faith; if there were such a bond, it would be harmful to our salvation because it would be harmful to our faith, since our faith would no longer be the sole source of our salvation.

As I have shown above in §§47, 48, 49, 50, it is actually true that that faith is incapable of being united to goodwill. Therefore one could say that it is a matter of foresight and predestination that Protestants tossed goodwill and good works so far away from their faith.

If Protestants had paired their faith with goodwill, it would have been like pairing a leopard with a sheep, a wolf with a lamb, or a hawk with a turtledove. (That faith is in fact described as a leopard in the Book of Revelation; see Revelation 13:2 and the explanation of that verse in *Revelation Unveiled* 572.)

What is a church without faith? What is faith without goodwill? What is a church, then, if it does not recognize the marriage that exists between faith and goodwill (see §48 above)? This marriage *is* the church itself; it *is* the new church that is now being established by the Lord.

69 As for the notion that when we are undergoing conversion we are like a log of wood, this is a teaching that the church of today acknowledges—in a great many words—as its own legitimate offspring. For example, it says that human beings are completely powerless in spiritual matters; see §15a, b, c. It says that in the process of being converted we are like a block of wood, a stone, or a statue; we cannot adapt or accommodate ourselves to grace; and we are like something that has no senses; see §15c, d. It says that we have only the power to move our bodies and attend public worship, where we can hear the Word and the gospel; see §15e. But it does say that the reborn, using power from the Holy Spirit, cooperate to some extent with him through the new capabilities and gifts they have received; see §15k. And many more teachings of this kind.

We are told that this is how we are in regard to our conversion and in regard to our repenting of the evil things we have done; but this is yet another offspring, hatched from the same egg and the same womb—namely, justification by faith alone. The purpose in their saying this is to remove altogether the works that we do and prevent our works from coming into any contact whatsoever with our faith. [2] Yet this attitude goes against the common sense we all have about repentance and about the process of our conversion; so they add the following statement to the others: "There is a great difference between baptized and unbaptized people. According to Paul's teaching, 'All those who have been baptized have put on Christ,' and are therefore truly reborn. They now have a 'freed choice.' For this reason they not only hear the Word of God but are also able to assent to it and embrace it with faith"; see §15m and the *Formula of Concord,* page 675.

I call on the wise to consider whether this last statement aligns at all with the others. Is it not a contradiction to say that all Christians go through their process of conversion like a log of wood or a stone, so much so that they cannot accommodate themselves to grace, and yet all Christians have been baptized and baptism entails being able not only to hear the Word of God but also to assent to it and embrace it with faith?

Therefore the comparing of a Christian to a log of wood or a stone must be eradicated from the churches in the Christian world. It must disappear, just as every strange phenomenon we see while we are asleep disappears when we wake up. It is highly offensive to human reason.

[3] In order to clarify what the new church teaches about our process of conversion, I would like to copy some words from an account of a memorable occurrence in *Revelation Unveiled*.

Surely we all see that every human being has the freedom to think about God and the freedom not to think about God. We all, then, have just as much freedom in spiritual matters as we do in civic and moral matters. The Lord grants all of us this freedom continually. We ourselves, then, are responsible and accountable for what we think.

It is this ability to choose what we think that makes humans human. It is the lack of this ability that makes animals animals. Therefore we possess the power to reform and regenerate ourselves seemingly on our own, provided we acknowledge at heart that this power comes from the Lord.

All who practice repentance are reformed and regenerated. We do this reforming and regenerating seemingly on our own. Even the ability to do things "seemingly on our own" comes from the Lord, because it is the Lord who gives us the will and the power and never takes them away from anyone.

It is absolutely true that we cannot contribute anything to our own regeneration. Nevertheless we were not created statues. We were created human beings so that we would be able to do this regenerating seemingly on our own but actually with the Lord's help. This responding through love and faith and forging a partnership with him is the one and only thing the Lord wants us to do for him.

Briefly put: Take action on your own, and yet trust that the Lord is helping you. This is what it means to take action seemingly on your own.

The ability to act on our own is not an attribute we were created with. Being able to act on one's own is an attribute that belongs to the Lord alone. He constantly grants it to us.

If we do what is good and believe what is true seemingly on our own, we become an angel of heaven. If we do what is evil and believe what is false (which are also things we do seemingly on our own), we become a spirit of hell. (The fact that this, too, is something we do seemingly on our own is attested to by our prayers asking to be protected from the Devil, so that he does not lead us astray and bring his evil into us.)

When we believe we are acting on our own, we are always at fault, whether what we do is good or evil. When we believe that we are acting *seemingly* on our own, we are not at fault. Whatever we believe we are doing on our own becomes a part of us. If it is something good, we view it as our property and claim it as our own, when in fact it belongs to God and comes from him. If it is something evil, we again view it as our property and claim it as our own, when in fact it belongs to the Devil and comes from him. [*Revelation Unveiled* 224:9–10]

For the purposes of this brief survey I will forego explaining a number of other things, including the point in the proposition above about adopting [false] principles of reason that are based on the teaching that we are justified by our faith alone and the teaching concerning the person of Christ, and using those principles to judge the uses and benefits of the sacraments (baptism and the Holy Supper); and the point that from the earliest centuries of Christianity until now, heresies have been leaping forth from a single source: the body of teaching based on the idea that there are three gods. These points will be presented and demonstrated in the work itself.

16

70 *The references in Matthew 24:3 to "the close of the age" and "the Coming of the Lord" that follows it mean the final state or the end of the church of today.*

Brief Analysis

71 In Matthew we read,

> The disciples came to Jesus and showed him the buildings of the Temple. Jesus said to them, "Truly, I say to you, not one stone will be left

here on another that will not be thrown down." The disciples said to him, "Tell us, when will these things be? Especially, what will be the sign of *your Coming and of the close of the age?*" (Matthew 24:1, 2, 3)

Today, learned clergy and well-educated lay people think that "the destruction of the Temple" refers to the Temple's destruction by Vespasian. They take "the Coming of the Lord" and "the close of the age" to mean the end or the death of this world. "The destruction of the Temple," however, refers not only to the Temple's destruction by Romans but also to the destruction of the church of today. "The close of the age" and the ensuing "Coming of the Lord" mean the end of the existing church and the establishment of a new church by the Lord. That whole chapter from beginning to end makes it clear that these terms have such a meaning; the sole topic is the successive states of decline and corruption within the Christian church leading up to its death, when it meets its end.

In a narrow sense, "the Temple" means the Temple in Jerusalem. In a broad sense, it means the Lord's church. In a broader sense, it means the angelic heaven. In the broadest sense, it means the Lord's human manifestation (see *Revelation Unveiled* 529). "The close of the age" means the end of the church; the end comes when the teaching from the Word has no truth left in it that has not been falsified and used up (see *Revelation Unveiled* 658, 676, 750). "The Coming of the Lord" means his Coming in the Word and his establishing a new church in place of the former church that has come to an end; this is clear from the Lord's words in the same chapter (Matthew 24:30–34) and in the two final chapters in the Book of Revelation (Revelation 21 and 22). In the last chapter there we read the following:

> I, Jesus, am the Root and the Offspring of David, the bright and morning star. The spirit and the bride say, "Come!" And those who hear, say, "Come!" And those who are thirsty, come. "Yes, I am coming quickly." Amen. Come, Lord Jesus! (Revelation 22:17, 20)

It is self-evident that the church is at an end when it has no more truths related to faith and no more good actions related to goodwill. False beliefs extinguish true teachings and evil lives consume good actions related to goodwill; where you find false beliefs, there you find evil lives, and where you find evil lives, there you find false beliefs. These points will be taken up individually in chapters of their own [§§74–76, 77–81].

72

Why has the information lain hidden that "the close of the age" means the end of this church? The reason is that where false ideas are being taught and people trust and honor that teaching as correct, it is impossible for them to realize that the church is coming to an end. False ideas are seen as true and true ideas as false. What is false then rejects what is true and blackens it the way ink blackens clear water or soot blackens a clean sheet of paper. This is because the most distinguished scholars of our age proclaim, and people generally believe, that the church is now standing in the crystal clear light of the gospel, when in reality the entire surface of the gospel is covered in thick darkness for them and white spots have covered the pupils of their eyes.

73   The statements in Matthew 24 and Mark 13 and Luke 21, which are similar to each other, are not describing the destruction of Jerusalem and its Temple; they are describing the successive changes of state the Christian church will go through in sequence, even to its final state, when it comes to an end. This will become clear in the work itself, where these chapters in Scripture will be explained.

In the meantime, the truth of this should be clear from the statements in the Gospels just mentioned:

> Then the sign of the Son of Humankind will appear and all the tribes of the earth will wail. They will see the Son of Humankind coming in the clouds of heaven with power and glory. He will send out his angels with a great sound of a trumpet, and they will gather his chosen people from one end of the heavens to the other. (Matthew 24:30, 31; Mark 13:26, 27; Luke 21:27)

As we all know, things like these were not heard or seen in Jerusalem when it was destroyed; today people believe they will occur instead at the time of the Last Judgment.

We read similar things in the Book of Revelation, which from beginning to end treats exclusively of the final state of the church:

> Behold, Jesus Christ is coming in the clouds, and all the tribes of the earth will wail over him. (Revelation 1:5, 7)

For an explanation of each of these expressions, see *Revelation Unveiled* 24–28. For what the tribes of the earth and their wailing means, see *Revelation Unveiled* 27, 348, 349.

17

The reference in Matthew 24:21 to "a great affliction such as has never **74**
existed since the world began and will never exist again" means an attack
by falsities and the resulting end—the devastation—of all truth in the
Christian denominations of today.

Brief Analysis

See §73 above for the point that Matthew 24 presents the Lord's predic- **75**
tions and descriptions of the successive states of decline and corruption
the Christian church would go through. As this chapter in Matthew
continues, there is a mention of false prophets yet to come who will
bring on an abomination of desolation (Matthew 24:11, 15). That chapter speaks of "a great affliction such as has never existed since the world
began until now and will never exist again" (Matthew 24:21). Clearly,
then, a "great affliction," both here and elsewhere in the Word, means
an attack by falsities against truth until no genuine truth drawn from
the Word, no truth that has not been falsified and completely ruined,
remains.

This has happened because the churches have not acknowledged
that God's unity in trinity and trinity in unity exist in *one* person rather
than in *three* persons. As a result they have based their church on a
mental picture of three gods, but an oral confession of one God. By
doing this they have separated themselves so far from the Lord that
they have completely lost the idea of any divinity in his human manifestation (see *Revelation Unveiled* 294). Yet the Lord in his human
manifestation is the divine truth itself and the divine light itself, as he
himself teaches comprehensively in his Word. This is why there is such
a great affliction today. As we will see in what follows [§§79–81], this
affliction has been caused primarily by the churches' teachings that
whether we possess faith (as the churches define it) or not is the sole
thing that determines whether we are justified and assigned Christ's
merit.

Seven chapters in the Book of Revelation deal specifically with this **76**
affliction or attack by falsities against the truth. This attack is meant by the

black horse and the pale horse that came forth from the scroll when the Lamb opened its seals (Revelation 6:5–8). This attack is meant by the beast that rose up from the abyss and made war against the two witnesses and killed them (Revelation 11:7 and following). This attack is meant by the dragon that stood before the woman who was about to give birth, waiting to devour her child, and persecuted her in the desert; there it sent forth water like a river from its mouth to swallow her up (Revelation 12). This attack is also meant by the beast from the sea, who had a body like a leopard, feet like a bear, and a mouth like a lion (Revelation 13:2). This attack is also meant by the three spirits that were like frogs, which came out of the mouths of the dragon, the beast, and the false prophet (Revelation 16:13). Finally, this attack is what is meant by the fact that after the seven angels poured out their bowls full of the wrath of God, which were the seven last plagues, onto the ground, into the sea, into the rivers and springs, into the sun, onto the throne of the beast, into the Euphrates, and finally into the air, there was a great earthquake unlike any that had occurred since the creation of humankind on the earth (Revelation 16). The "earthquake" means that the church is turned upside down; this is brought about by people teaching what is false and falsifying the truth.

Similar things are meant by the following passage as well:

> The angel put forth his sickle and harvested the vineyard of the earth, and threw it into the great winepress of the wrath of God. And the winepress was trampled, and blood came out, up to the horses' bridles, for one thousand six hundred stadia. (Revelation 14:19, 20)

"Blood" here means truth that has been falsified.

There are many other examples in those seven chapters; see, if you wish, the explanations of those chapters and the accounts of memorable occurrences that come after them.

18

77 *The statement in Matthew 24 "After the affliction of those days, the sun will be darkened, the moon will not give its light, the stars will fall from heaven, and the powers of the heavens will be shaken" (Matthew 24:29)*

means that at the last time of the Christian church, when its end is
imminent, it will have no love, no faith, and no knowledge of what is
good or what is true.

Brief Analysis

The prophetic Word includes a number of statements about the sun, [78]
the moon, and the stars that are similar to this statement in Matthew
24:29. For example, in Isaiah:

> Behold, the fierce day of Jehovah is coming. The *stars* of the heavens
> and their *constellations* will not shine their light. The *sun* will be dark-
> ened in its rising, and the *moon* will not make its light shine. (Isaiah
> 13:9, 10)

In Ezekiel,

> When I extinguish you, I will cover the heavens and darken the *stars.*
> I will cover the *sun* with a cloud, and the *moon* will not give its light. I
> will bring darkness upon your land. (Ezekiel 32:7, 8)

In Joel,

> The day of Jehovah is coming, a day of darkness; the *sun* and the *moon*
> will be darkened and the *stars* will withhold their light. (Joel 2:1, 2, 10)

> The *sun* will be turned into darkness and the *moon* into blood before
> the great day of Jehovah comes. (Joel 2:31)

> The day of Jehovah is at hand in the valley of decision; the *sun* and the
> *moon* have been darkened. (Joel 3:14, 15)

In the Book of Revelation,

> The fourth angel sounded, and a third of the *sun* was struck, [a third of
> the *moon,*] and a third of the *stars;* and a third of the day did not shine.
> (Revelation 8:12)

Also in the Book of Revelation,

> The *sun* became black as sackcloth of goat hair and the *moon* became
> like blood. (Revelation 6:12)

The topic of all the Old Testament passages here is the final times of the Jewish church, which occurred when the Lord came into the world. The passages from Matthew and the Book of Revelation are similar, but they deal with the final times of the Christian church, when the Lord is going to come again, but this time in the Word, which contains him and is him. For this reason, immediately after the statement in Matthew 24:29 the following passage occurs: "Then the sign of the Son of Humankind will appear, coming in the clouds of the heavens" (Matthew 24:30).

In these passages "the sun" means love, "the moon" means faith, and "the stars" mean knowledge of what is good and what is true. "The powers of the heavens" mean all three of these things as the sources of strength and stability for the heavens, where angels are, and the churches, where people are.

Gathering all the above together into one meaning, then, they refer to the fact that at the last time of the Christian church, when its end is imminent, it will have no more love, no more faith, and no more knowledge of what is good or what is true.

(For a demonstration that the sun means love, see *Revelation Unveiled* 53, 54, 413, 796, 831, 961; that the moon means faith, see *Revelation Unveiled* 53, 332, 413, 533; that the stars mean knowledge of what is good and what is true, see *Revelation Unveiled* 51, 74, 333, 408, 413, 954.)

79 As predicted, there is such great darkness in the Christian denominations of today that during the day there is no light from the sun, and during the night there is no light from the moon or the stars. The one and only cause of this is *the teaching that we are justified by our faith alone.* This teaching presents faith as the sole means of being saved, although it also asserts that no one has ever seen a sign that this faith is flowing in, progressing, making a home, working, or achieving any results in us. We are told that this faith has nothing to do with our obeying the law of the Ten Commandments, or our goodwill, good works, repentance, or efforts to live a new life—these actions have no impact whatever on our faith; instead these actions arise spontaneously, but are completely useless for preserving our faith or gaining us salvation.

This teaching holds that faith of this kind grants the reborn, or those who have received their badge of freedom, exemption from being subject to the law. In addition, Christ covers up their sins before God the Father. God the Father then forgives those sins (since he has not seen them) and bestows upon these people renewal, sanctity, and eternal life. These thoughts and many others like them lie at the core of this teaching.

Its outward features remain outside this core; they are the activities of goodwill, good works, acts of repentance, and the following of the law, which are actually extremely valuable. Christian authorities present them, however, as lowly, humble servants; faith is the lady of the house. As servants, they are allowed to follow along behind her, but not to have any contact with her. Nevertheless, because these preachers and teachers are aware that lay people are counting on these activities as well as their faith to save them, they take great care to ensure that these topics are included in their sermons and conversations. They even pretend to combine these activities with, and find a place for them in, the process of justification. They do so, however, only to please the ears of the crowd and to keep their own oracular pronouncements from sounding too much like riddles or sorcery.

In order to provide evidence from the *Formula of Concord* for what I have just said (for more on the *Formula of Concord,* see §9 above), I will add the following references. My purpose is to keep you from thinking that I am hurling unfounded accusations. **80**

The works enjoined by the second tablet of the Ten Commandments are civic in nature and form a part of our external worship that we can do on our own. It is foolish to dream, though, that they make us just before God (pages 84, 85, 102).

Good works must be completely excluded from the article on justification through faith (pages 589, 590, 591, 704–708).

Our good works play absolutely no part in our justification (pages 589, 702; appendix, pages 62, 173).

Our good works do not preserve faith or salvation in us (pages 590, 702; appendix, page 174).

Our repentance, too, plays no role in our being justified by faith (pages 165, 320; appendix, page 158).

Repentance consists in merely calling on God, confessing the gospel, giving thanks, obeying our leaders, and doing our jobs (pages 12, 198; appendix, pages 158, 159, 172, 266).

Our living a new life, too, has nothing to do with our process of being made just (pages 585, 685, 688, 689; appendix, page 170).

Our efforts to practice a new kind of obedience play no part in our faith or our being justified (pages 90, 91, 690; appendix, page 167).

Those who are reborn are not under the law; they are liberated from slavish adherence to it. They are in the law but under grace (page 722 and elsewhere).

The sins committed by the reborn are covered up by Christ's merit (pages 641, 686, 687, 719, 720, not to mention many other similar passages).

It is important to recognize that all Protestants, including both Lutherans and Calvinists, have similar teachings regarding justification by faith alone; see §§17, 18 above.

81 Astoundingly, the teaching that faith is the only thing that justifies us occupies every square inch throughout the entire Protestant world; that is, within the clergy it rules as virtually the only theology. This position is what all candidates for the ministry eagerly learn, consume, and absorb in college. Then, as if they were people inspired with heavenly wisdom, they teach that position in their churches and publish it in their books. Through it they pursue and achieve the name, reputation, and glory of having superior erudition. Because of it they are given diplomas, fellowships, and awards. And all this goes on, despite the fact that as a result of that teaching alone the sun today is darkened, the moon is deprived of its light, and the stars of the heavens have fallen, that is, have been destroyed.

I have been given absolute proof that the teaching that faith assigns us justice has so blinded human minds today that they do not want, and are therefore virtually unable, to see any divine truth in the light of the sun or in the light of the moon. They can see it only in the light of a fireplace by night. I can therefore make this assertion: If divine truths about the true partnership between goodwill and faith, about heaven, about the Lord, and about the eternal happiness that comes from him were to be written in silver letters and sent down from heaven, people who believe that we are justified by faith alone would not even consider them worth reading. The complete opposite would happen, though, if a paper asserting that faith alone makes us just were to be sent up from below.

We also read in the *Formula of Concord* that the article concerning justification by faith alone, or concerning the justice that we acquire through faith, is the most important of all Christian teachings, and that works of the law must be completely excluded from this article (pages 17, 61, 62, 72, 89, 683; appendix, page 164).

19

The goats mentioned in Daniel and Matthew mean people who are **82** *devoted to the modern-day view that faith is what justifies us.*

Brief Analysis

In Daniel we read the following: **83**

> In a vision I saw a ram that had two tall horns, the taller of which rose up behind [the other]. With its horn the ram pushed westward, northward, and southward and became enormous.
>
> Then I saw a goat that came from the west across the surface of the whole earth; it had a horn between its eyes. It charged at the ram in the fury of its strength, broke the ram's two horns, and cast the ram to the ground and trampled it. The large horn of the goat was broken, and four horns sprang up in its place. A little horn came out of one of them, which grew tremendously toward the south, toward the dawn, and toward the beautiful [land], and even to the host of the heavens, and cast down to earth some of the host and some of the stars, and trampled them. The goat even exalted itself toward the Leader of the Host, and took the daily offerings away from him and cast down the dwelling place of his sanctuary, because it cast truth to the ground. And I heard a holy one saying, "How long will this vision last concerning the daily offerings and this destructive sinning, the trampling of the holy place and the host?" And he said, "Until the evening [and] the morning: then the holy place will be set right." (Daniel 8:2–14)

It is obvious that this vision foretells states the church is going to go through in the future, since it says that the goat took the daily offerings away from the Leader of the Host, that it cast down the dwelling place of his sanctuary, and that it cast truth to the ground. This is also clear from the fact that a holy one said, "How long will this vision last concerning the trampling of the holy place and the host?" and is told this would continue until the evening [and] the morning: then the holy place will be set right. "The evening [and] the morning" means the end of the old church, when a new church arises.

84   In Matthew we read the following:

> Then the Son of Humankind will say to the goats on the left, "Depart from me, because I was hungry and you did not give me anything to eat. I was thirsty and you did not give me anything to drink. I was a stranger and you did not take me in. I was naked and you did not clothe me. I was sick and in prison and you did not visit me." These will go away into everlasting punishment. (Matthew 25:41–46)

It is very clear that the goats and the sheep mentioned here have the same meaning as the goat and the ram in Daniel. What evidence is there that "the goats" mean people who are devoted to the modern-day belief that faith is what justifies us? This point is made clear by the fact that the sheep are mentioned in connection with a list of actions that reflect goodwill, and they are said to have done these actions; then the goats are mentioned in connection with the same list of actions, but they are said *not* to have done them, and this is why they are condemned.

People who embrace the modern-day view that faith is what justifies us neglect to do good works, because they deny that good works have anything to do with our salvation or the church. When goodwill is laid aside, the good works that come from it slip our minds; we never even think of them or make any effort to remember them from the law of the Ten Commandments.

It is a general principle of religious practice that if we are not willing and doing good actions, then we are willing and doing evil actions. The opposite is also true: if we are not willing and doing evil actions, then we are willing and doing good actions. "The goats" are the people who take the first approach just mentioned. "The sheep" are the people who take the second approach.

If "the goats" in that passage had meant everyone who is evil, the list would have covered the evil things they had done; instead it lists the acts of goodwill that they did not do.

85   Experiences in the spiritual world have made it very plain to me that "the goats" mean precisely people like these. In the spiritual world we see the same things that exist in the physical world. We see houses and mansions. We see parks and gardens—the gardens contain trees of all different kinds. We see fields of crops and fields that have recently been plowed. We see meadows and lawns. We also see flocks and herds. All these things are the same there as they are here on the physical planet Earth. The only difference is that the things on Earth have a physical origin but the things in the spiritual world have a spiritual origin.

In that world I have often seen sheep and goats. I have seen them battling with each other, much like the battle described in Daniel 8. I have seen goats with horns that curved forward and that curved backward. I have seen goats furiously charging at sheep. I have seen goats with two horns, and goats with four horns, violently butting sheep with them. When I have looked around to see what this meant, I have seen people arguing with each other about whether faith is united to goodwill or is entirely separate from it.

These experiences have made it clear to me that the modern-day view that faith is what justifies us (which is a faith that is by definition completely separate from goodwill) is a goat; and faith that is united to goodwill is a sheep.

The goats mentioned in Zechariah have the same meaning:

86

> My wrath blazes against the shepherds, and I will execute judgment upon the *goats.* (Zechariah 10:3)

Likewise, the goats mentioned in Ezekiel:

> Behold, I am judging between one flock animal and another, between *rams* and *goats.* Is it too little for you to have eaten up the good pasture? Will you also trample what remains of the food with your feet? You attack all the weak *sheep* with your horns until you have scattered them. Therefore I will save *my flock,* so that it will no longer be prey. (Ezekiel 34:17, 18, 21, and following)

20

Adamant devotees of the modern-day view that faith is what justifies **87** *us are depicted in the Book of Revelation as the dragon, its two beasts, and the locusts. This belief (when strongly held) is depicted there as the*

great city that is spiritually called Sodom and Egypt, where the two
witnesses were killed, and as the pit of the abyss from which the locusts
came forth.

Brief Analysis

88 Seven chapters in the Book of Revelation concern the corrupt state of
the Protestant churches, and two chapters concern the corrupt state of the
Roman Catholic churches. This and the now condemned condition of
these churches has been shown in the explanation of the Book of Revelation titled *Revelation Unveiled*—and shown not with idle guesswork but
with overwhelming evidence.

The *dragon* in Revelation 12 means Protestants who split God into
three and the Lord into two and who separate goodwill from faith by saying that their faith is something spiritual and effective for our salvation
but goodwill is not. See *Revelation Unveiled* 532–565 and the *memorable
occurrence* immediately following in §566.

The same people are also described as the two beasts, one of which
rises up out of the sea and the other out of the land in Revelation 13. See
Revelation Unveiled 567–610 and the *memorable occurrence* immediately
following in §611.

The same people are also described as the locusts that come out of the
pit of the abyss in Revelation 9. See *Revelation Unveiled* 419–442.

This belief (when adamantly clung to) is depicted in Revelation 11 as
the great city that is spiritually called Sodom and Egypt, where the two
faithful witnesses were killed. See *Revelation Unveiled* 485–530, especially
§§500–503, and the *memorable occurrence* in §531.

This belief is also depicted, in Revelation 9, as the pit of the abyss,
from which smoke came out like the smoke of a great furnace, darkening
the sun and the air, and from which locusts then came forth. See *Revelation Unveiled* 421–424.

89 The exact meaning of the pit of the abyss is "dragon faith"—that is,
faith that originates in the idea of three gods, lacks any notion that Christ's
human nature was divine, and is hailed as the faith that alone justifies us,
regenerates us, brings us to life, sanctifies us, and saves us. To convince me
completely of this to the point of absolute certainty, I have been allowed
to look down into that abyss and talk to the people who are there. I have

also seen the locusts that come out of that pit. From this eyewitness experience I have given a description in *Revelation Unveiled* of the pit and the abyss. Because nothing is better for establishing certainty than an eyewitness account, I will copy my account of that experience here, as follows.

The pit, which is like the opening to a furnace, is found in the southern region. The abyss below it stretches far toward the east. There is light in the pit and the abyss, but if light from heaven is let into them, they become very dark. For this reason the pit is closed at the top.

In the abyss you see temporary housing that looks as if it is made of brick, with holes in the walls. It is divided into many little cells. Each cell contains a table with paper and some books on it, and a person sitting at it. All of these are people who, in the world, had become adamant supporters of justification and salvation by faith alone. They characterized goodwill as an act of mere earthly morality, and good works as just things we do in our civic lives to earn ourselves rewards in the world. If people do them for the sake of their salvation, however, these writers condemn that, some of them very harshly, on the grounds that such actions are tainted with human reason and will.

All the people in the abyss were learned and well-educated when they were in the world. Some are theoretical philosophers and Scholastic philosophers; these are the ones accorded the highest esteem by others in the abyss.

What happens to them over time is as follows. When they are first sent there, they sit in the little cells at the front. As they lend reinforcement to faith and exclude works of goodwill they leave the first locations and move to cells that are farther east. This relocating happens again and again until they reach the end, where people use the Word to support those teachings. Because by that point they cannot help but falsify the Word, their housing disappears and they find themselves in a desert.

There is another abyss below the first. It contains people who had become similarly adamant about justification and salvation by faith alone, but who in their spirits had also denied the existence of God and at heart had laughed at the holy teachings and practices of the church. The only things people do there are argue, tear each other's clothes, climb on tables, kick at each other, and attack each other with insults. Because they are forbidden to harm each other, they hurl threats and shake their fists at each other.

90   The dragon means adamant supporters of the modern-day view that faith is what justifies us. To make me convinced and certain of this, I was given the opportunity to see thousands and thousands of such people gathered into an assembly. From a distance they looked like a dragon with a long tail, which was covered with spikes like a bramble bush; the spikes symbolize falsities.

On another occasion I saw a dragon that was even larger. With its back lifted up, it reached its tail toward heaven in an effort to drag the stars down. The stars in that world symbolize truths.

21

91   *Unless the Lord establishes a new church, no one can be saved. This is the meaning of the statement in Matthew 24:22 "Unless those days were cut short no flesh would be saved."*

Brief Analysis

92   "Cutting those days short" means bringing the modern-day church to an end and establishing a new church. As mentioned before, Matthew 24 is about the successive states of decline and corruption within the Christian church leading up to its close and end, and about the Lord's Coming, which happens after that.

The reason why no flesh would be saved if those days were not cut short is that the faith of the modern-day church is based on the idea of three gods, and no one who has that *idea* can get into heaven. Therefore no one with that *faith* can get into heaven either, because the idea of three gods is present in every detail of it. For another thing, that faith contains within itself no life from acts of goodwill. As I have shown in §§47–50 above, it is incapable of being united to goodwill or producing any fruit in the form of good works.

There are two things that build a heaven within us: truths that lead to faith and good actions that come from goodwill. Truths that lead to faith bring us the presence of the Lord and show us the way to heaven. Good actions that come from goodwill give us a partnership with the Lord and bring us into heaven. There we are each brought into a light that accords with how much desire we have for what is true, and into a warmth that accords with how much desire we have for what is good. Faith in its essence is a desire for what is true, and goodwill in its essence is a desire for what is good. The church is a marriage between faith and goodwill; see §48 above. And heaven and the church are united. Faith, goodwill, and heaven (as I have demonstrated fully in the preceding pages) do not exist in the churches that are built on faith alone.

In the spiritual world I have talked a number of times with people who say faith alone makes us just. I said that their teaching is wrong and also absurd; it brings on spiritual complacency, blindness, sleep, and night; and it is eventually lethal to the soul. I urged them to give it up. **93**

I received the response, "Why stop? This is the sole area in which the clergy can claim to be better educated than lay people."

I replied that in that case they must be viewing a superior reputation as their goal, not the saving of souls. Since they have applied the truths in the Word to their own false principles, which means they have contaminated them, they are the angels of the abyss called Abaddons and Apollyons (Revelation 9:11; those names mean people who have destroyed the church by completely falsifying the Word; see *Revelation Unveiled* 440, and the *memorable occurrence* in §566 there).

They replied, "What? Since we know the mysteries of that teaching, we are oracles. We give answers from that faith as if it were a sacred shrine. We are not Apollyons; we are Apollos!"

Irritated at that, I said, "If you are Apollos you are also leviathans. The leaders among you are coiled leviathans, and the followers among you are uncoiled leviathans. God will punish you with his sword, great and strong (Isaiah 27:1)."

They just laughed at that.

(For the meaning of being punished with and perishing by a sword, see *Revelation Unveiled* 52.)

Here is the great secret as to why no flesh could be saved if the Lord were not establishing a new church. As long as the dragon and its crew stay in the world of spirits where they went when they were thrown down from heaven, no divine truth united to divine goodness can get across from the Lord to people on earth without being perverted or annihilated. Therefore there is no salvation. This is what the Book of Revelation means when it says, **94**

> The dragon was thrown down onto the earth and its angels were thrown with it. Woe to those who live on the earth and in the sea, because the

Devil has come down to them in a giant rage. It persecuted the woman who had given birth to a son. (Revelation 12:9, 12, 13)

It was after the dragon was thrown down into hell (Revelation 20:10) that John saw a new heaven and a new earth and saw the holy New Jerusalem coming down from God out of heaven (Revelation 21:1, 2, and following). (For what "the dragon" means and who "the dragons" are, see §§87–90 above.)

22

95   *"The one who sat on the throne said, 'Behold, I am making all things new'; and said to me, 'Write, because these words are true and faithful'" (Revelation 21:5). This statement in the Book of Revelation means our examining and rejecting the tenets of faith of the modern-day church and God's revealing and our accepting the tenets of faith of the new church.*

Brief Analysis

96   The scriptural quotation just above is what the one who sat on the throne, that is, the Lord, said to John when John saw the New Jerusalem coming down from God out of heaven. (The New Jerusalem means the new church, as the next point will demonstrate [§§99–101].)

The reason why the falsities in the tenets of faith of the modern-day church have to be examined and rejected first before the truths in the tenets of the new church are revealed and accepted is that the two systems do not agree at any point or at any time. The tenets of the modern-day church are built on faith as their foundation, and yet no one knows whether anything essential to the church lies within that faith or not. The essential elements of the church, which are things that unite themselves to a faith in one God, are goodwill, good works, repentance, and a life in accordance with divine laws. Because these four, together with faith, affect and move both our will and our thoughts, they unite us to the Lord and the Lord to us. Since none of these essential elements plays any part in the faith espoused by the modern-day church at the moment when that faith comes into us—the moment referred to as "the act of justification"—it is completely impossible to know whether that faith is in us or not. Therefore it cannot even be known whether that faith is anything real or is just an idea. We are told that in the moment [of acquiring faith] we are like a stone or a block of wood and that when it comes to receiving faith, we are entirely unable to will, think, cooperate, or adapt or accommodate ourselves to it; see §15c, d. None of us can even guess, then, let alone know, whether that faith exists within us or not. We do not know whether it is like a flower in a painting we own or like a flower in a field inside us. We do not know whether it is like a bird flying past us or like a bird nesting in us. We ask what signs and indications might lead us to the answers to these questions. The reply is that we may know this from the goodwill, good works, repentance, and following of the law that occur in us once we have faith. We have nevertheless also been told that there is no bond whatever between faith and these things. I leave it to the wise to investigate whether a *lack* of a bond can be a sign that testifies to anything! For example, our faith (we are told) is not preserved or maintained by the actions just listed; see §121, m.

The conclusion to be drawn is that nothing of the church has anything to do with the modern-day faith. Therefore the modern-day faith is not indeed anything; it is just a notion that there is such a thing. Given that this is the nature of that faith, it deserves to be rejected; in fact, since it contains not a single attribute of a church, it rejects itself.

It is very different with the tenets or teachings of the new church, though. All of them are essential elements. Heaven and the church are present in each one of them. The goal toward which they aim is for us to be in the Lord and for the Lord to be in us, according to his own words in John 14:20; 15:4, 5, 6. Simply put, the [true] Christian church *is* this type of partnership with the Lord.

From the mere handful of points just made, we can clearly see the meaning of the Lord's words:

> The one who sat on the throne said, "Behold, I am making all things new"; and said to me, "Write, because these words are true and faithful." (Revelation 21:5)

Why did the Christian world latch onto a faith that has distanced itself from everything good and true in heaven and in the church even to the point of completely separating itself from them? The sole reason is this: people split God into three, and did not believe that the Lord God the Savior is one with God the Father and therefore did not turn directly to the Lord.

Yet the Lord alone, in his human manifestation, is the divine truth itself, "which is the Word that was God with God and the true light that enlightens everyone, and the Word that became flesh" (John 1:1, 2, 9, 14). In other passages the Lord himself testifies that he is the truth itself and the light itself. For example, he says,

> I am the light of the world. (John 8:12; 9:5)

> While you have the light, believe in the light, so that you may become children of the light. I have come into the world as a light so that anyone who believes in me will not remain in darkness. (John 12:36, 46)

In the Book of Revelation,

> I am the Alpha and the Omega, the Beginning and the End, the First and the Last, the bright and morning star. (Revelation 22:13, 16)

In Matthew,

> When Jesus was transfigured, his face shone like the sun and his clothing became like light. (Matthew 17:2)

All this clarifies how that imaginary faith came into the world. It came about because people did not turn to the Lord. From the attestation of all my experiences in heaven I can declare with absolute certainty that it is impossible to derive even a single theological truth that is genuinely true from any source other than the Lord alone. It is as impossible to get truth from anywhere else as it is to sail from Britain or the Netherlands to the Pleiades, or to ride a horse from Germany to Orion in the sky.

23

99 *The New Jerusalem, which is the topic of Revelation 21 and 22, and is there called the bride and wife of the Lamb, is the new church that is going to be established by the Lord.*

Brief Analysis

100 The New Jerusalem coming down from God out of heaven (Revelation 21) means the new church. For one thing, Jerusalem was the largest city in the land of Canaan. The Temple was there. The altar was there. The sacrifices were performed there. It was the center for divine worship. Three times a year every male in the entire country was commanded to come worship there. Another reason is that the Lord was in Jerusalem and taught in its Temple; it was there that he glorified his human manifestation. For these reasons "Jerusalem" means the church.

[2] The fact that Jerusalem means the new church is abundantly clear in what the prophets of the Old Testament say about the new church that the Lord is going to establish, which they refer to as Jerusalem. I will present only passages in which the fact that *Jerusalem* means the church is easy to see for anyone who has the ability to reason inwardly. We will limit ourselves, then, to just the following.

> Behold, I am creating *a new heaven and a new earth;* the former ones will not be remembered. Behold, I am *going to create Jerusalem* as a rejoicing and her people as a gladness, so that I may rejoice over *Jerusalem* and be glad about my people. Then the wolf and the lamb will feed together; they will do no evil in all my holy mountain. (Isaiah 65:17, 18, 19, 25)

> For Zion's sake I will not be silent and for *Jerusalem's* sake I will not rest until her justice goes forth like radiance and her salvation burns like a lamp. Then the nations will see your justice and all monarchs will see your glory, and a new name will be given you that the mouth of Jehovah will utter. And you will be a crown of beauty [in the hand of Jehovah] and a diadem of the kingdom in the hand of your God. Jehovah will be well pleased with you and your land will be married. Behold, your salvation will come. See, his reward is with him. And they will call them a holy people, the redeemed of Jehovah; and you will be a city sought out, not deserted. (Isaiah 62:1–4, 11, 12)

> Wake up! Wake up! Put on your strength, O Zion. Put on your beautiful garments, *O Jerusalem,* holy city. No more will the uncircumcised or the unclean come into you. Shake yourself from the dust, rise up, and sit [in a higher place], *Jerusalem.* The people will acknowledge my name on that day, because I am the one saying, "Here I am!" Jehovah has comforted his people; he has redeemed *Jerusalem.* (Isaiah 52:1, 2, 6, 9)

> Rejoice, O daughter of Zion! Be glad with all your heart, O daughter of *Jerusalem!* The King of Israel is in your midst. Do not fear evil anymore. He will be glad over you with joy; he will rest in your love; he will

rejoice over you with singing. I will give you a name and praise among all the peoples of the earth. (Zephaniah 3:14–17, 20)

Thus says Jehovah your Redeemer, who says to *Jerusalem,* "You will be inhabited." (Isaiah 44:24, 26)

Thus says Jehovah: "I will return to Zion and dwell in the midst of *Jerusalem. Jerusalem* will be called the city of truth, and the mountain of Jehovah Sabaoth will be called the holy mountain." (Zechariah 8:3; see also 8:20–23)

Then you will know that I am Jehovah your God, dwelling on Zion, my holy mountain. *Jerusalem* will be holy. And on that day it will happen that the mountains will drip with new wine and the hills will flow with milk; and *Jerusalem* will abide from generation to generation. (Joel 3:17–21)

On that day the branch of Jehovah will be beautiful and glorious. And it will happen that those remaining in Zion and those left in *Jerusalem* will be called holy—all who are written as alive in *Jerusalem.* (Isaiah 4:2, 3)

At the very last of days the mountain of the house of Jehovah will be established on the top of the mountains. Teaching will go forth from Zion and the Word of Jehovah from *Jerusalem.* (Micah 4:1, 2, 8)

At that time they will call *Jerusalem* the throne of Jehovah, and all nations will gather at *Jerusalem* because of the name of Jehovah. They will no longer follow the stubbornness of their own evil heart. (Jeremiah 3:17)

Look upon Zion, the city of our appointed feasts! Your eyes will see *Jerusalem* as a peaceful abode, a tabernacle that will not be taken down; its tent pegs will never be removed and its cords will not be torn away. (Isaiah 33:20)

Not to mention other passages, such as Isaiah 24:3; 37:32; 66:10–14; Zechariah 12:3, 6–10; 14:8, 11, 12, 21; Malachi 3:2, 4; Psalms 122:1–7; 137:4, 5, 6.

[3] *Jerusalem* in the passages just quoted does not mean the Jerusalem where Jews once lived, but the church of the Lord to come. This is clear from every detail of the description in the passages: for example, the point that Jehovah God is going to create a new heaven and a new

earth, including a Jerusalem; that this Jerusalem is going to be a crown of beauty and a diadem of the kingdom; that it is going to be called "holy," "the city of truth," "the throne of Jehovah," "a peaceful abode," "a tabernacle that will not be taken down"; that the wolf and the lamb will feed together there; and we are told that the mountains there will drip with new wine, the hills will flow with milk, and it will abide from generation to generation. This is also clear from what we are told of the people there, that they are holy, they have all been written as alive, and they are to be called "the redeemed of Jehovah."

[4] What is more, all these passages indicate that only at the time of the Lord's Coming, especially his Second Coming, [but not before,] will "Jerusalem" be the way these passages describe it. Before that, Jerusalem is not married; that is, it has not yet become the bride and wife of the Lamb, which is how the New Jerusalem is described in the Book of Revelation.

In Daniel, *Jerusalem* means the church of today, the former [Christian] church. The beginning of this church is described in the following words.

> Know and understand: from [the time] the Word goes forth that Jerusalem must be restored and built until [the time of] Messiah the Leader will be seven weeks. Then after sixty-two weeks the street and the trench will be restored, but in troublesome times. (Daniel 9:25)

The end of the church of today is described in the following words from the same chapter:

> In the end desolation [will fly in] on a bird of abominations; even to the close and the cutting down, it will drip steadily upon the devastation. (Daniel 9:27)

The final stages of the church of today are also what the following words of the Lord in Matthew are referring to:

> When you see that the abomination of desolation foretold by the prophet Daniel is standing in the holy place, let those who read note it well. (Matthew 24:15)

Evidence that *Jerusalem* in the passages above does not mean the Jerusalem where Jews once lived is found in the passages in the Word in which we are told that Jerusalem has already been completely destroyed or is going to be in the future. See Jeremiah 5:1; 6:6, 7; 7:17, 18, and following; 8:6, 7, 8, and following; 9:10, 11, 13, and following; 13:9, 10, 14; 14:16; Lamentations 1:8, 9, 17; Ezekiel 4:1 to the end; 5:9 to the end; 12:18, 19; 15:6, 7, 8; 16:1–63; 23:1–40; Matthew 23:37, 38; Luke 19:41–44; 21:20, 21, 22; 23:28, 29, 30; besides many other passages. See also the passages where Jerusalem is referred to as Sodom (Isaiah 3:9; Jeremiah 23:14; Ezekiel 16:46, 48; and elsewhere).

 The church belongs with the Lord. Because of the spiritual marriage between what is good and what is true, the Lord is called Bridegroom and Husband and the church is called Bride and Wife. Christians know this from the Word, especially from the following passages in it.

> John said of the Lord, "*The bridegroom* is the one who has *the bride.* The friend of *the bridegroom,* who stands and hears him, rejoices because of *the bridegroom's* voice." (John 3:29)

> Jesus said, "As long as *the bridegroom* is with them, *the children of the wedding* cannot fast." (Matthew 9:15; Mark 2:19, 20; Luke 5:34–35)

> I saw the holy city, the New Jerusalem, coming down from God out of heaven, prepared as *a bride adorned for her husband.* (Revelation 21:2)

> The angel said to John, "Come, I will show you *the bride, the wife of the Lamb,*" and from a mountain he showed him the city, the holy Jerusalem. (Revelation 21:9, 10)

> The time for *the Lamb's wedding* has come; *his bride* has prepared herself. Blessed are those who are called to the *marriage supper of the Lamb.* (Revelation 19:7, 9)

> "I am the Root and the Offspring of David, the bright and morning star." And *the spirit and the bride* say, "Come!" And those who hear, say, "Come!" And those who are thirsty, come. Those who wish to, take the water of life freely. (Revelation 22:16, 17)

24

102 *There is no way in which we can simultaneously hold the views of the new church and the views of the former church on faith; if we did hold* *both these views at once, they would collide and cause so much conflict that everything related to the church would be destroyed in us.*

Brief Analysis

The reason why there is no way to simultaneously hold the views of the new church and the views of the former church (that is, the modern-day church) regarding faith is that the two positions do not overlap by a third or even a tenth.

103

In Revelation 12 the faith of the former church is portrayed as a dragon (see §§87–90 above) and the faith of the new church is portrayed as a woman clothed with the sun, who had a crown of twelve stars on her head. The dragon persecuted her and spewed water like a flood at her in an effort to carry her away by it. These two views cannot coexist in the same city, much less in the same household or the same mind. If they were to come together, the only possible outcome would be that the woman would be constantly exposed to rage and insanity from the dragon, and would constantly fear that the dragon would devour her son. After all, we read in Revelation 12 that the dragon stood before the woman, when she was about to give birth, in order to devour her child. After the woman gave birth, she fled into the wilderness (Revelation 12:1, 4, 6, 14–17).

The faith held by the former church is a faith of the night; human reason has no experience of it at all. This is why we are told that we are to hold our intellect under obedience to faith. In fact, we do not even know whether it is within us or outside of us. The human will and human reason have nothing to do with it.

For that matter, goodwill, good works, repentance, the law of the Ten Commandments, and a number of other things that actually exist in the human mind have nothing to do with it (see §§79, 80, 96, 97, 98). The faith of the new church, however, forms a partnership and a marriage covenant with all the things just mentioned. As a result, this faith lives in the warmth of heaven; and because it does, it also lives in heaven's light. It is a faith of the light.

A faith of the night and a faith of the light cannot live together any more than an owl and a dove can live together in one nest. The owl would lay its eggs there, and the dove would lay its eggs. After incubation, both sets of chicks would hatch, and then the owl would tear apart the dove's chicks and feed them to its chicks. (Owls are voracious.)

The faith of the former church cannot live with the faith of the new church because the two are completely incompatible. The faith of the former church is descended from the idea that there are three gods (see §§30–38 above); the faith of the new church, though, is descended from the idea that there is one God. And because the two are completely incompatible as a result, it is inevitable that if they lived together in us they would collide and cause so much conflict that everything related to the church would be destroyed in us. We would fall into such a state of spiritual madness or else spiritual unconsciousness that we would hardly know what the church was or whether such a thing even existed.

Consequently, people who are deeply committed to the faith of the old church are incapable of embracing the faith of the new church without endangering their own spiritual lives, unless they have first rejected the teachings of the former faith one by one and have uprooted that former faith along with all its live offspring and unhatched eggs (meaning tenets). What these tenets are like has been shown earlier in this work, especially in §§64–69.

104   A similar thing would happen to us if we were to embrace the faith of the new church but also hold onto the faith of the former church regarding the assignment of the Lord's justice or merit, since from the latter concept as from a root all the tenets of the former church have risen up like shoots.

If this were to happen, it would be like people escaping from three of the dragon's heads but entangling themselves in the other four. It would be like running away from a leopard but stumbling onto a lion. It would be like climbing out of a dry pit only to fall into a water-filled pit and drown.

(The truth of this statement will be further shown after the discussion of the next proposition [§§109–113], where the topic of being assigned spiritual credit or blame is taken up.)

25

105   *Roman Catholics today are not at all aware that their church once embraced concepts of the assigning of Christ's merit to us and of our justification by faith in that. These concepts lie completely buried beneath their external rituals of worship, which are many. Therefore if Catholics* *give up some of their external rituals, turn directly to God the Savior Jesus Christ, and take both elements in the Holy Eucharist, they are better equipped than Protestants to become part of the New Jerusalem, that is, the Lord's new church.*

Brief Analysis

When the leaders and priests of the Roman church are ordained into the ministry, they swear to uphold the decrees of the Council of Trent. This is clear from the papal bull issued by the Roman pope Pius IV, on November 13, 1564, which presents the formula to be followed when declaring a sworn profession of faith:

> I with a firm faith believe and profess all and every one of the things contained in that creed which the holy Roman Church makes use of. I likewise undoubtingly receive all other things delivered and declared by the sacred Canons and ecumenical Councils, and *particularly by the holy Council of Trent*—so help me God.

In that same oath they constrain themselves to believe and profess the specific teachings sanctioned by the Council of Trent regarding the assigning of Christ's merit to us and our justification by faith in that, as is clear from the following words in that same papal bull:

> I embrace and receive all and every one of the things which have been defined and declared in the holy Council of Trent concerning original sin and justification.

The contents of those teachings can be reviewed in the material collected from the Council of Trent in §§3, 4, 5, 6, 7, 8 above.

These principles established in the Council of Trent lead to the following conclusions.

Roman Catholics before the Reformation had exactly the same teachings as Protestants did after it regarding the assigning of Christ's merit to us and our being justified by faith in that; the only difference was that Catholics united this faith to goodwill or good works (see §§19, 20 above).

The leading reformers—Luther, Melanchthon, and Calvin—retained the Roman Catholic dogmas regarding the assigning of Christ's merit to us and our being justified by faith. They kept those views as they had

106

been, and still were at the time, among Roman Catholics. The reformers separated goodwill or good works from that faith, however, and declared that faith alone saves, for the purpose of clearly differentiating themselves from Roman Catholics with regard to the essentials of the church, which are faith and goodwill (see §§21, 22, 23 above).

The leaders of the Protestant Reformation do indeed describe good works as an appendage to faith and even an integral part of faith, but they say we are passive in the doing of them, whereas Roman Catholics say we are active in the doing of them. There is actually strong agreement between Protestants and Catholics on the subjects of faith, works, and our rewards (see §§24–29 above). Clearly, then, these beliefs used to be as important to Roman Catholics as they are now to Protestants.

107 Nevertheless, today these beliefs have been so thoroughly wiped out among Roman Catholics that they scarcely know the least thing about them. These beliefs have been forgotten not because they were overturned by papal decree but because they were covered over by external facets of worship. In general these are adoring the vicar of Christ, calling on the saints, and venerating images; they are especially things that affect our physical senses with an impression of holiness, such as the Mass, which is conducted in a language people do not understand, the vestments, the candles, the incense, and the spectacular processions; also the mysteries surrounding the Eucharist.

Although the early Roman church believed that faith justifies us through assigning us the merit of Christ, the external facets just listed and many others like them have moved this concept out of sight and removed it from memory, as if it were something buried in the ground, covered with a large stone, and guarded by monks so that it will not be dug up and brought back to mind. The danger in its being brought back to mind is that it would undermine people's belief in the monks' supernatural power to forgive their sins, and justify, sanctify, and save them; and that would end the monks' status as holy, their dominance over others, and their quest for wealth.

108 The *first reason* why Roman Catholics are better equipped than Protestants to become part of the New Jerusalem (that is, the new church) is this: The belief that we are justified by being assigned Christ's merit, which is wrong and cannot live alongside the faith of the new church (see §§102–104), has been wiped out among Roman Catholics, and should be completely eradicated. This belief is firmly fixed in Protestants, however, as if it were carved into their being. It is the chief teaching in their church.

The *second reason* is that Roman Catholics have more of an idea than Protestants that there is divine majesty in the Lord's human manifestation. This is abundantly clear in the extremely sacred way in which Roman Catholics venerate the Host.

The *third reason* is that Roman Catholics see goodwill, good works, repentance, and the effort to live a new life as essential to salvation; the new church, too, considers them essential. Protestants who are committed to faith alone, though, have a very different view. They see these as playing a nonessential role or even no role at all in our faith; they see them as contributing nothing to our salvation.

These are three reasons why Roman Catholics, if they turn to God the Savior himself directly rather than indirectly and if they take both elements in the Holy Eucharist, are better equipped than Protestants to receive a living faith in place of a dead one and be led by the Lord, through the agency of his angels, to the gates of the New Jerusalem (the new church) and brought in shouting for joy.

[The Assignment of Christ's Merit]

The notion that Christ's righteousness or merit is assigned to us permeates the entire theological system in today's Protestant Christian world. It is because of this assigning that our faith (which Protestant Christianity takes to be the sole means of being saved) can be referred to as our righteousness before God; see §11d. The assigning that happens as a result of our faith clothes us with the gifts of righteousness, much as a newly crowned monarch is adorned with royal insignia.

109

In reality, however, this assigning accomplishes nothing if all it involves is that we are called righteous. It does no work within us; it only flows into our ears, unless this assigning of righteousness includes an actual transfer of righteousness to us through some process of its being shared with us and incorporated into us. This conclusion follows from the list of things that are claimed to be the effects of this assigning: our sins are forgiven, and we are regenerated, renewed, sanctified, and therefore saved. This claim is clearer still from the fact that Christ is said to dwell in us and the Holy

Spirit is said to work in us as a result of that faith; and therefore we are not only considered to be righteous but actually are righteous. It is not just the gifts of God that reside in the reborn, but because of their faith, Christ too and in fact the entire holy Trinity dwells in them as his temple; see §15l. Both we as people and the works we do should be called, and should be, completely righteous; see §14e.

From these points it undoubtedly follows that "the assigning of Christ's righteousness" must mean an actual transfer of righteousness to us through some process of its being incorporated into us, through which we become a partaker in it.

Now, because this concept of assigning is the root, the start, and the foundation of faith and of all the work faith does for our salvation, and because it is therefore the sanctuary and shrine at the center of all Christian church buildings today, it is important to add as an appendix [to this work] an examination of this notion of assigning, presented point by point as follows.

1. After we die we are all assigned either blame for the evil or else credit for the goodness to which we have devoted ourselves.
2. It is impossible to incorporate one person's goodness into another person.
3. Given that this is impossible, it is an imaginary faith to believe that Christ's righteousness or merit is assigned to or transferred into us.

110   1. *After we die we are all assigned either blame for the evil or else credit for the goodness to which we have devoted ourselves.* In order to make this clear, I will break it down into the following pieces: (a) We all have our own individual life. (b) Our life stays with us after we die. (c) At that point, evil people are assigned blame for the evil that constituted their life, and good people are assigned credit for the goodness that constituted theirs.

(a) *We all have our own individual life.* This is well known. Each of us is differentiated from everyone else. There is an unending variety among people, and nothing about us is identical; so we each have our own unique selfhood.

This becomes very clear when we consider human faces. Not one face is absolutely identical to any other face, nor could there ever be two identical faces to eternity, because no two minds are alike, and the face reflects the mind. Our face, as they say, is a mirror of our mind, and our mind is formed and shaped by our life.

If we did not have our own unique life (just as we have our own unique mind and our own unique face), after death we would not have a life that was differentiated from anyone else's. In fact, there would be no heaven, since heaven consists of an unending variety of people. The form heaven takes is possible only because of all the varieties of souls and minds, arranged into a design in such a way that they all work together as one. They work together as one due to the one whose life is present within each of them, like the soul within a human being. If this were not the case, heaven would fall apart because that form would collapse. The Lord is the one who is the source of life for each and every person there and is the force that holds the entire form together.

[2] (b) *Our life stays with us after we die.* The church recognizes this from statements in the Word. For example, "The Son of Humankind is going to come; then he will repay all people according to their deeds" (Matthew 16:27). "I saw books opened. All were judged according to their works" (Revelation 20:12, 13). "In the day of judgment, God will repay all according to their works" (Romans 2:6; 2 Corinthians 5:10). The works according to which we will be repaid are our life; our life produces these works, and they are done in accordance with our life.

For many years now I have been allowed to be among angels and talk to new arrivals from the physical world. As a result I can testify that all of us are explored there to see what kind of life we have; the life we formed in the world stays with us to eternity. I have spoken with people who lived centuries ago, whose lives I knew about from historical accounts, and recognized that they fit the description.

I have been told by angels that it is impossible for our life to be changed after death, because it is organized around the love and faith we had, and the things we did as a result. If our life were to be changed, it would tear apart that whole structure, and that could never happen. Changes in that structure are possible only while we are alive in the physical body; such changes are completely impossible in the spiritual body once our physical body has been cast off.

[3] (c) *At that point, evil people are assigned blame for the evil that constituted their life, and good people are assigned credit for the goodness that constituted theirs.* Being assigned blame for evil after we die is not the same as being accused or charged or declared guilty or judged [by someone else], the way we would be in the physical world. We are assigned blame by the evil itself that is within us. Evil people freely choose to leave good people, since the two types of people cannot coexist. The pleasures involved in

loving what is evil are completely opposite to the pleasures involved in loving what is good. In the spiritual world, each type of person exudes an atmosphere of what pleases her or him, just as different types of plants on earth give off their own unique odor. There, these exhalations are not absorbed or covered up by the physical body the way they used to be in the physical world; instead they flow forth freely from the individual's love into the spiritual atmosphere. Evil is sensed there as having its own smell; therefore the presence of evil itself is what accuses us, charges us, declares us guilty, and judges us—not in the presence of some judge but in the presence of anyone who is devoted to goodness. This is what the "assigning of blame for evil" means.

The assigning of credit for goodness happens in much the same way. We are assigned credit for goodness if in the world we acknowledged that everything good about us was and is from the Lord and none of it came from ourselves. People who acknowledge this undergo a preparation first and are then brought into the inner pleasures associated with the goodness they love. After that a pathway opens up for them, leading to a community in heaven where the angels take delight in things that are in harmony with what the new arrivals take delight in. This is the Lord's doing.

III   2. *It is impossible to incorporate one person's goodness into another person.* The evidence for this can be seen if it is laid out in the following order. (a) Every one of us is born with evil. (b) We are brought into goodness by going through the process of being regenerated by the Lord. (c) Our regeneration is occasioned by our believing in the Lord and living by his commandments. (d) Therefore one person's goodness cannot be transferred and incorporated into and credited to another person.

(a) *Every one of us is born with evil.* The church is well aware of this. The church tradition holds that this evil is something we inherit from Adam; in actual fact, though, it comes from our parents. Each of us derives a particular nature from our parents, which takes the form of certain tendencies. Both experience and reason teach that this is true. Similarities to parents are obvious in the faces, characters, and behaviors of their children and also grandchildren. As a result, families are widely recognizable, and we can even discern certain characteristics of their lower minds. Therefore the evils that the parents have become involved with are passed down to subsequent generations in the form of a tendency to engage in those evils. This is the origin of the evils we are born with.

(b) *We are brought into goodness by going through the process of being regenerated by the Lord.* The Lord's words in John 3:3, 5 make it clear that there is a process of regeneration and that if we do not undergo this process we cannot come into heaven. In the Christian world it is impossible to miss that the process of being regenerated is a process of being purified from evils and beginning a new life. Reason is able to see this as well, provided it accepts that every one of us is born with evil, and that evil cannot be washed or wiped away with soap and water as if it were dirt, but can be washed away by our recovery of wisdom.

(c) *Our regeneration is occasioned by our believing in the Lord and living by his commandments.* For the five principles of regeneration, see §§43, 44 above. The following are taken from that list: We must abstain from doing things that are evil—they belong to the Devil and come from the Devil. We must do things that are good—they belong to God and come from God. We must turn to the Lord so that he can lead us to live this way.

You should all take the time to consider whether goodness could possibly become ours in any other way; and without goodness, we have no salvation.

(d) *Therefore one person's goodness cannot be transferred and incorporated into and credited to another person.* It follows from what has just been said that the process of regeneration is what makes our spirits new, and that this process is occasioned by our believing in the Lord and living by his commandments.

Surely everyone can see that this process of being made new can occur only over time, much the way a seed takes root, grows into a tree, and comes to full maturity in stages. People who think differently about the process of being regenerated and made new know nothing about the human condition. They also do not realize that evil and good are complete opposites, and that what is good can only be implanted to the extent that evil has been removed. They are also not aware that as long as we are involved in evil we have an aversion to any goodness that is truly and intrinsically good. Therefore if one person's goodness were to be transferred and incorporated into another person who was devoted to evil, it would be like throwing a lamb in with a wolf or tying a pearl to a pig's snout. Clearly, then, it is impossible to incorporate one person's goodness into another person.

3. *Given that this is impossible, it is an imaginary faith to believe that Christ's righteousness or merit is assigned to or transferred into us.* In §110 **112**

above, the point was made that we are all assigned blame for the evil or else credit for the goodness to which we have devoted ourselves. This makes it clear that if this concept of "assigning" is taken to mean the transfer and incorporation of one person's goodness into another person, it is imaginary thinking.

In our world rewards are in one sense transferable by people. A benefit that is owed to parents can be reassigned to their children; a favor that is owed to a client can be redirected to the client's friends. The good qualities and actions that earned the reward, though, cannot be transferred into these other people's souls; the reward can only outwardly be attached to people.

No such reassignment of benefit is possible in regard to people's spiritual lives. Spiritual life has to be planted in us. As mentioned just above [§111], if it is not planted in us as a result of our living by the Lord's commandments, we stay involved in the evil we were born with. Before spiritual life is planted in us, nothing good can affect us. As soon as any goodness touches us it immediately either rebounds and bounces off us like a rubber ball hitting a rock or else is swallowed up like a diamond thrown in a swamp.

People who have not been reformed are like a panther or a horned owl in spirit; they can be compared to brambles and stinging nettles. People who have been regenerated, though, are like a sheep or a dove; they can be compared to olive trees and grapevines. Please consider, if you will, how panther-people could possibly be converted into sheep-people, or horned owls into doves, or brambles into olive trees, or stinging nettles into grapevines, through any assignment of divine righteousness, if "assignment" here means any kind of transfer. Is it not true that in order for that conversion to take place, the predatory nature of the panther and the horned owl and the damaging nature of the brambles and the stinging nettles would first have to be removed and something truly human and harmless implanted in their place? The Lord in fact teaches in John 15:1–7 how this transformation occurs.

113   To these things I will add the following: There is a saying in the church that no one can fulfill the law, especially since someone who breaks one of the Ten Commandments breaks them all [James 2:10–11; Matthew 5:19]. But this formulaic saying does not mean what it seems to. The proper way to understand it is that people who purposely or deliberately behave in a way that is contrary to one commandment in effect behave contrary to the rest, because doing something [against one commandment] purposely and deliberately is the same as completely denying that that behavior is sinful. And people who deny and reject the very idea of sin see nothing wrong with breaking the other commandments.

As everyone is surely aware, just because someone is a *fornicator* does not mean that he or she is, or wants to be, a murderer, thief, or false witness. People who commit *adultery* purposely and deliberately, though, see no value in any religious practice, and therefore see nothing wrong even with murders or acts of theft or false witness; they abstain from doing such things not because doing so would be sinful but because they are afraid of the law and any negative effect on their reputation.

Similarly, if people break another of the Ten Commandments purposely or deliberately, they break the rest as well, because they do not consider anything to be sinful.

[2] Much the same is true for people who are devoted to doing good things that come from the Lord. If such people abstain from one evil on the grounds that that evil is sinful, they abstain from all evils (provided that both their will and their intellect are engaged in the process, that is, they abstain from that evil purposely and deliberately). The effect is even greater if they intentionally abstain from more than one evil. As soon as we abstain purposely or deliberately from any sinful evil, we are held by the Lord in a resolution to abstain from the rest as well. Therefore if it happens that because we did not realize what was going on or because we were overwhelmed with physical desire, we do something evil, it is not held against us. It was not something we planned to do, and we do not support what we did.

We develop this resolve if we examine ourselves once or twice a year and recover from an evil we find in ourselves. If we never examine ourselves, we do not develop this resolve.

[3] I may reinforce this point as follows. In the spiritual world I have come across many people who had shared a similar lifestyle when they were in the physical world. They all dressed in fashionable clothing, enjoyed fine dining, took profit from their business, went to the theater, told jokes about lovers as if they themselves were lustful, and many other things of the kind. Yet for some of these people the angels labeled their behaviors as evil and sinful, whereas for others the angels did not. The angels declared the former guilty and the latter innocent. Upon being asked why this was, since the people had done the same things, the angels replied that they had evaluated all the people on the basis of their plans, intentions, and purposes and distinguished them accordingly. Those whose purpose

excused them, the angels excused, and those whose purpose condemned them, the angels condemned, since the goal of all who are in heaven is to do good, and the goal of all who are in hell is to do evil. From this it becomes clear who is assigned blame for sin and who is not.

114   To these points I will add two *memorable occurrences* taken from *Revelation Unveiled.*

The first memorable occurrence. I was suddenly overcome with a deathly illness. My whole head felt worse and worse. A poisonous smoke was blowing in from the great city that spiritually is called Sodom and Egypt (Revelation 11:8). I was half dead and in severe pain. I thought I was about to die. I lay in bed in that condition for three and a half days. My spirit developed this sickness, and then my body came down with it as well.

Then I heard voices around me saying, "Look, he is lying dead in the street of our city—the one who was preaching that we should repent so that our sins would be forgiven and [that we should worship] only Christ the human being."

They asked some of the clergy, "Is he worthy of burial?" (We read that the same thing happened to the two witnesses who were killed in that city; see Revelation 11:8, 9, 10.)

The clergy replied, "No. Let him lie there as a spectacle."

They kept going away and coming back to mock me.

And I am telling the truth when I say that this happened to me at the very time that I was explaining the eleventh chapter of the Book of Revelation.

Then I heard more serious words from the people who had been mocking me—especially these: "How can repentance be practiced apart from faith? How can Christ the human being be adored as God? Given that we are saved for free without our deserving it at all, what then do we need except faith alone—the faith that God the Father sent the Son to take away the damnation of the law, to credit us with his own merit, to justify us before the Father, to absolve us from our sins, and then to give us the Holy Spirit, who activates every good thing within us? Aren't these points in accordance with Scripture and also with reason?"

The crowd of bystanders applauded these statements.

[2] I heard all this but was unable to respond because I was lying there almost dead.

After three and a half days, however, my spirit regained its health. In the spirit I went from that street into the city, and I said again, "Practice repentance and believe in Christ, and your sins will be forgiven and you will be saved. If you do not, you will perish. The Lord himself preached that we must repent in order for our sins to be forgiven, and that we must believe in him. He commanded the disciples to preach the same message. Surely the dogma of your faith leads to utter complacency about the way you live!"

"What are you babbling about?" they replied. "The Son has made satisfaction. The Father has assigned us the Son's merit and has justified us for the reason that these are our beliefs. We are now led by the spirit of grace. What sin could there be within us? What death could there be among us? Do you grasp this Good News, you preacher of sin and repentance?"

Then a voice from heaven said, "Surely the faith of someone who has not practiced repentance is nothing but a dead faith. The end has come, the end has come upon you who are complacent, guiltless in your own eyes, justified by your own faith—devils!"

At that moment a chasm suddenly opened up in the middle of the city and spread outward. The houses were falling in on each other and the people were swallowed up. Soon water bubbled up from the great hole and flooded what was already devastated.

[3] After they sank to a lower level and were seemingly covered in water, I wanted to know what their situation was like in the depths. A voice from heaven told me, "You will see and hear."

Then the water that had seemingly flooded them disappeared from before my eyes. (Water in the spiritual world is a correspondence that appears around people who have false beliefs.) I saw the people in a sandy place at a great depth, where there were piles of stones. They were running between the piles of stones and loudly bemoaning their having been cast out of their great city.

They were shouting and wailing, "Why has this happened to us? We are clean, pure, just, and holy because of our faith."

Others were saying, "Surely through our faith we have been cleansed, purified, justified, and sanctified."

Still others were asking, "Hasn't our faith made it possible for us to be seen and esteemed by God the Father and the whole Trinity, and to be declared before angels, as clean, pure, righteous, and holy? Haven't we been reconciled, atoned for, ritually purged, and therefore absolved, washed, and wiped free of our sins? Didn't Christ take away the damnation of the law? Why then have we been thrown down here like the damned? We did hear from a bold proclaimer of sin in our great city, 'Believe in Christ and practice repentance.' But didn't we believe in Christ when we believed in his merit? Didn't we practice repentance when we confessed that we were sinners? Why then has this happened to us?"

[4] A voice was then heard from the side: "Are you aware of any sin in yourselves? Have you ever examined yourselves, and then abstained from any evil because it is sinful against God? If you do not abstain from sin, then you are still devoted to it; and sin is the Devil. You, then, are the people of whom the Lord spoke when he said, 'You will then begin to say, "We ate and drank with you. You taught in our streets." But he will say, "I tell you, I do not know you, where you are from. Depart from me, all you workers of wickedness"' (Luke 13:26, 27). Matthew 7:22, 23 is also about you. Therefore go away, each to your own place. Do you see the holes leading to those caves? Go in there, and each of you will be given your own work to do, and food in accordance with your work. If you don't go in, your hunger will drive you in."

[5] After that a voice from heaven came to some people who were up at the level of the ground but were outside the city (see Revelation 11:13). The voice said loudly, "Beware! Beware of associating with people like that. Don't you understand that evils that are called sins and acts of wickedness make us unclean and impure? How can you be cleansed and purified from them except by active repentance and by faith in the Lord God the Savior? Active repentance is examining yourselves, recognizing and admitting to your sins, accepting that you are at fault, confessing them before the Lord, begging for his help and power in resisting them, stopping doing them, and living a new life. All this is to be done as if you were doing it on your own. Do this once or twice a year when you are about to take Holy Communion. Afterward, when the sins for which you are at fault recur, say to yourselves, 'We do not want these, because they are sins against God.' This is actual repentance.

[6] "Surely you can all recognize that if you do not examine yourselves and see your sins, you remain in them. From birth you find all evils delightful. It feels good to take revenge, to be promiscuous, to steal, and to slander. Because they feel good you overlook them. If someone happens to point out to you that they are sins, you make excuses for them because they feel good. You use false arguments to defend them and convince yourselves that they are not sins, and you stay in them. And afterward you do those evil things more than you did before, to the point where you no longer know what sin is or even whether there is such a thing.

"It is different, however, for people who actively go through a process of repentance. The evils that they recognize and admit to [in themselves] they call sins. They therefore begin to abstain and turn away from them. Eventually they begin to feel the pleasure of those evils as unpleasant. The more this happens, the more they see and love what is good, and eventually even feel delight in it, which is the delight that the angels in heaven feel. Briefly put, the more we put the Devil behind us, the more we are adopted by the Lord and are taught, led, held back from what is evil, and kept in what is good by him. This is the pathway from hell to heaven; there is no other way."

[7] It is amazing that Protestants have such a deep-seated resistance, antipathy, and aversion to active repentance. Their reaction to it is so strong that they cannot force themselves to do self-examination, to see their sins, and to confess them before God. It is as if they are overcome by horror as soon as they form the intention to do it. I have asked many Protestants in the spiritual world about this, and they all said that it is completely beyond their strength. When they heard that Catholics practice this, that is, that they examine themselves and openly confess their sins to a monk, the Protestants were profoundly amazed, especially since the Protestants themselves could not do this even in secret before God, although they had been commanded, just as the Catholics had been, to do this when they were about to take the Holy Supper. Some people in the spiritual world investigated why this was, and discovered that faith alone was what had led to such an impenitent state and such an attitude of heart. Then those Protestants were allowed to see that Catholics are saved if they turn to Christ and worship him, and no longer worship but only honor the leaders of their churches.

[8] After that we heard a kind of thunder, and a voice speaking from heaven and saying, "We are amazed. Say to the gathering of Protestants, 'Believe in Christ and practice repentance, and you will be saved.'"

So I said it.

I added, "Clearly, *baptism is a sacrament of repentance* and therefore introduction into the church. What else do godparents promise for the child being baptized but that she or he will renounce the Devil and all his works? Clearly, *the Holy Supper is a sacrament of repentance* and therefore introduction into heaven. Doesn't the priest say to those about to take it that they absolutely have to practice repentance first? Clearly, *the Ten Commandments are the universal teaching of the Christian church; they urge repentance.* Isn't it true that the six commandments on the second tablet say, 'You are *not* to do this and that thing that is evil,' not, 'You *are* to do this and that thing that is good'? Therefore you are capable of knowing that the more we abstain from what is evil, the more we love what is good; and that before that, we do not know what good is, or even what evil is."

115 *The second memorable occurrence.* Once an angel said to me, "Do you want to see clearly what faith and goodwill are, and therefore what faith separated from goodwill is, and what faith united to goodwill is? I will express it in visual terms for you."

"Please do!" I answered.

The angel said, "Instead of faith and goodwill, think of light and heat, and you will see them clearly. Faith in its essence is truth that relates to wisdom. Goodwill in its essence is affection that relates to love. In heaven, truth related to wisdom is light and affection related to love is heat. The light and heat that angels live in are, in essence, exactly this. As a result, you can clearly see what faith is when it is separated from goodwill and what it is when it is united to goodwill.

"When faith is separated from goodwill, it is like the light in winter. When faith is united to goodwill, it is like the light in spring. The light in winter, which is a light separated from heat, is united to coldness; therefore it completely strips trees of their leaves, kills grass, makes ground as hard as rock, and freezes water. Light in spring, which is a light united to heat, causes trees to grow, first producing leaves, then flowers, and finally fruit; it also unlocks and softens the ground so that it produces grass, plants, flowers, and shrubs; and it melts ice, so that water flows from its sources again.

"The situation with faith and goodwill is absolutely identical. Faith separated from goodwill kills everything. Faith united to goodwill brings everything to life. This killing and this bringing to life are vividly visible in this spiritual world of ours, because here faith *is* light and goodwill *is* heat. Where faith has been united to goodwill there is a paradise of gardens, flower beds, and lawns; the more united faith and goodwill are, the more pleasing the gardens are. Where faith has been separated from goodwill, there is not even grass; the only greenness comes from thorns and brambles."

At that point there were some members of the clergy not far away. The angel called them "justifiers and sanctifiers of people through faith alone" and also "arcanists." We said the same things to the members of the clergy and added enough proof that they could see that what we said was true. But when we asked them, "Isn't that so?" they turned away and said, "We didn't hear you." So we cried out to them and said, "Then keep listening to us," but they put both hands over their ears and shouted, "We don't *want* to hear you!"

Closing Thought from Jeremiah 7:2, 3, 4, 9, 10, 11

Stand in the gate of the house of Jehovah and proclaim this word there. "Thus says Jehovah Sabaoth, the God of Israel: 'Make your ways and your deeds good. Do not put your trust in lying words, saying, "The temple of Jehovah, the temple of Jehovah, the temple of Jehovah are these." Are you going to steal, kill, commit adultery, and swear falsely, and then come and stand before me in this house that bears my name and say "We are delivered" when you are doing all these abominations? Has this house become a den of thieves? Behold I, even I, have seen it,' says Jehovah."

Concluding Appendix

116 *T*HE *faith of the new heaven and the new church in universal form is* this: The Lord from eternity, who is Jehovah, came into the world to gain control over the hells and to glorify his own human nature. If he had not done this, not one mortal could have been saved; those who believe in him are saved.

[2] I say "in universal form" because this concept is universal to the faith and something universal to the faith is going to be present in each and every aspect of it. It is universal to the faith to believe that God is one in essence and in person, to believe that in God there is a trinity, and to believe that the Lord God the Savior Jesus Christ is God. It is universal to the faith to believe that if the Lord had not come into the world not one mortal could have been saved. It is universal to the faith to believe that the Lord came into the world to separate hell from the human race, and that he accomplished this by repeatedly doing battle with hell and conquering it. In this way he gained control over it, put it back into the divine design, and made it obey him. It is universal to the faith to believe that he came into the world to glorify the human nature he took on in the world, that is, to unite it to its divine source. Having gained control over hell and having glorified his human nature, he keeps hell in its place, under obedience to him forever. Since neither of these achievements could have happened except by allowing his human nature to be tested, including even the ultimate test, the suffering on the cross, therefore he underwent that experience. These are universal points of faith regarding the Lord.

[3] For our part, it is universal to the Christian faith that we believe in the Lord, for our believing in him gives us a partnership with him, and through this partnership comes salvation. To believe in him is to have confidence that he saves; and because only those who live good lives can have such confidence, this too is meant by believing in him.

117 *The faith of the new heaven and the new church in a specific form is* this: Jehovah God is love itself and wisdom itself, or goodness itself and truth itself. As divine truth, or the Word, which was "God with God," he came down and took on a human manifestation for the purpose of forcing everything in heaven, everything in hell, and everything in the

92

church back into the divine design. The power of the Devil, that is, hell, had become stronger than the power of heaven, and on earth the power of evil had become stronger than the power of goodness; therefore total damnation stood threatening at the door. [2] By means of his human manifestation, which was divine truth, Jehovah God lifted this pending damnation and redeemed both people and angels. Afterward, in his human manifestation, he united divine truth to divine goodness. In this way he returned to the divine nature that he had had from eternity, together with the human manifestation, which had been glorified. These things are meant by this statement in John: "The Word was with God, and the Word was God. And the Word became flesh" (John 1:1, 14). And in the same Gospel, "I came forth from the Father and have come into the world. Again, I leave the world and go to the Father" (John 16:28). From all this it is clear that if the Lord had not come into the world no one could have been saved.

The situation today is similar. Therefore if the Lord does not come into the world again in the form of divine truth, which is the Word, no one can be saved.

[3] For our part, the specifics of faith are these: (1) There is one God, the divine trinity exists within him, and he is the Lord God the Savior Jesus Christ. (2) Believing in him is a faith that saves. (3) We must abstain from doing things that are evil—they belong to the Devil and come from the Devil. (4) We must do things that are good—they belong to God and come from God. (5) We must do these things as if we ourselves were doing them, but we must believe that they come from the Lord working with us and through us.

The first two points have to do with faith; the second two have to do with goodwill; and the fifth has to do with the partnership between goodwill and faith, the partnership between the Lord and us. (On these points, see also §44 above.)

Three Memorable Occurrences
Taken from *Revelation Unveiled*

THE first memorable occurrence. Once as I was explaining chapter 20 in the Book of Revelation and was meditating on the dragon, the beast, and the false prophet, an angelic spirit appeared to me and asked what I was meditating on. I said, "The false prophet."

118

The angelic spirit said, "I will take you to the place where the spirits meant by the false prophet are." He added, "They are the same spirits portrayed in chapter 13 of the Book of Revelation as the beast from the earth who had two horns like a lamb, but who spoke like a dragon."

I followed the angelic spirit. To my surprise I saw a crowd with church leaders in the center of it. The leaders were teaching that nothing saves us except faith in Christ's merit and that works are good things to do, but not for our salvation. They were also proclaiming that works need to be taught from the Word so as to put lay people, especially simple ones, on a leash so that they obey their civic leaders and feel compelled from within by religion to practice moral goodwill.

[2] Then one of them saw me and said, "Do you want to see our shrine? It has a sculpture in it that portrays our faith."

I went and saw it. It was magnificent! In the center of the shrine there was a statue of a woman dressed in scarlet clothes. She had a gold coin in her right hand and a chain of pearls in her left.

Both the statue and the shrine, however, were projected images. Hellish spirits have the ability to portray magnificent things using projected images. They do it by closing off the inner levels of our mind and opening only its outer levels.

When I realized that the statue and the shrine were conjured up through sorcery I prayed to the Lord. Suddenly the inner levels of my mind were opened. Then instead of a magnificent shrine, I saw a house that was full of cracks from the roof all the way to the foundation. Nothing in it was solidly connected. Instead of the woman, I saw a dummy hanging in the house, which had the head of a dragon, the body of a leopard, the feet of a bear, and the mouth of a lion. It was exactly like the beast from the sea described in Revelation 13:2. Instead of the floor, there was a swamp that contained thousands of frogs. I was told that under the swamp there was a great hewn stone; and beneath it the Word lay deeply hidden.

[3] Seeing this I said to the sorcerer, "Is this your shrine?"

"It is," the sorcerer said.

Just then, though, the sorcerer's inner sight opened up as well. The sorcerer saw the same things I was seeing and loudly shouted, "What is this? Where did this come from?"

"It came from the light of heaven," I said, "which has disclosed the true quality of each form here, including the quality of your faith, which has been separated from spiritual goodwill."

Immediately the east wind came up and blew away the shrine with the sculpture. It dried up the swamp and exposed the stone that had the Word lying underneath it.

Then a warm, springlike breeze blew in from heaven. To my surprise I then saw a tent in that same place, a very simple one in its outer form.

Angels who were with me said, "Look, it is Abraham's tent just as it was when the three angels came to him to announce that Isaac was going to be born [Genesis 18:1, 2, and following]. The tent looks simple to the eye, but as the light of heaven flows in, it becomes more and more magnificent."

The angels were then granted the ability to open the heaven where spiritual angels live—the angels who have wisdom. In the light that flowed in from that heaven, the tent looked like the Temple in Jerusalem. When I looked inside, I saw that the foundation stone under which the Word had been hidden was now covered in precious stones. From the precious stones a kind of lightning was flashing onto walls that had reliefs of angel guardians on them, giving the angel guardians beautifully different colors.

[4] As I was feeling awestruck by these sights, the angels said, "You are about to see things that are even more miraculous." They were then granted the ability to open the third heaven where heavenly angels live— the angels who have love. As a result of the light that flowed in from that heaven, the entire temple disappeared. In its place I saw the Lord alone, standing on the foundation stone, which *was* the Word. He looked much the way he had when seen by John in Revelation chapter 1.

Yet because holiness then filled the inner realms of the angels' minds so that they felt an overwhelming urge to fall forward on their faces, suddenly the channel of light from the third heaven was closed by the Lord and the channel of light from the second heaven was reopened. As a result, the earlier appearance of a temple, and also a tent, returned. The tent was in the temple.

These experiences illustrated what Revelation 21 means when it says, "Behold, the tent of God is among people, and he will dwell with them" (Revelation 21:3); and when it says, "I saw no temple in the New Jerusalem, because the Lord God Almighty is its temple, and the Lamb" (Revelation 21:22).

The second memorable occurrence taken from Revelation Unveiled. One time just after I woke up from sleeping I fell into a deep meditation on *God.* Looking up I saw above me in heaven an oval of intensely shining

119

light. As I fixed my gaze on the light, it gradually receded toward the sides and merged into the periphery [of my vision].

Then, behold, heaven opened up to me! I saw some magnificent things, and angels standing in a circle on the south side of the opening, talking to each other. Because a burning desire came over me to hear what they were saying, I was allowed to hear it—first the sound of it, which was full of heavenly love; then the conversation itself, which was full of the wisdom that goes with that love.

They were having a conversation about *the only God,* about *being in partnership with God,* and about *the salvation* that results. What they were saying was ineffable—most of it could not be expressed in the words of any earthly language. Several times before, however, I had been in gatherings of angels in heaven itself, and had been able to join in their conversation because I was then in a state similar to theirs. This enabled me to understand them now, and to select from their discussion a few points that could be expressed in a rational way using the words of earthly language.

[2] They were saying that *the underlying divine reality is united, uniform, absolute, and undivided.* They said that the same is true of the divine essence, because the underlying divine reality is the divine essence, and that the same is also true of God, because the divine essence that is the underlying divine reality is God. They used spiritual images as illustration.

They said, "The underlying divine reality cannot be divided into many entities, each of which possesses an underlying divine reality, and still remain united, uniform, absolute, and undivided. Otherwise each separate entity would think on its own from its own separate underlying divine reality. If it also happened to be concurrently of the same mind as the others, there would be a number of deities in agreement; there would not be one God. Agreement, or the consensus of many, each one acting on its own or by itself, is not an attribute of one God but of many."

They did not say "gods" because they were unable to. It was suppressed by the light of heaven that shaped their thought and was the context in which their conversation took place. They also said that when they tried to utter the word "gods" and to describe each one as a person by himself, the effort to say that immediately veered off toward "one," and in fact toward "the one only God."

[3] They added, "The underlying divine reality is a reality in itself, not from itself, because if it were from itself, that would imply an underlying

reality that existed in itself from some prior underlying reality. It would mean there was a god from a god, which is not possible. What comes from God is called 'divine,' but it is not called 'God.' What is 'a god from God,' what is 'an eternally begotten god from God,' and what is 'a god emanating from an eternally begotten god from God' except words utterly devoid of heavenly light?"

Later on they said, "The underlying divine reality, which in itself is God, is *uniform*—and uniform not just in a simple way but in an infinite number of ways. It is uniform from eternity to eternity. It is uniform everywhere, and it is uniform with everyone and in everyone. (It is the condition of the recipient that causes all the variety and variability in reception.)"

[4] The angels demonstrated the *absoluteness* of the underlying divine reality, which in itself is God, as follows: "God is the Absolute, because he is absolute love and absolute wisdom, or to put it another way, he is absolute goodness and absolute truth. As a result, he is life itself. If these qualities were not absolute in God they would never exist in heaven or in the world, because they would be relatively nonexistent compared to the Absolute. Every quality is what it is because it comes from the Absolute, both as its source and as its point of reference.

"The Absolute (meaning the underlying divine reality) has no specific location. It is with those and in those who are in specific locations, depending on how receptive they are. Love and wisdom, goodness and truth, and the life these qualities give are absolute in God; in fact, they are God himself. A specific location cannot be attributed to them, and neither can a progression from place to place as the source of their omnipresence—they are not in a particular place. For this reason the Lord says he is in the midst of people [Matthew 18:20]; and he is in them and they are in him [John 6:56; 14:20; 15:4, 5].

[5] "Nevertheless, no one can comprehend God as he is in himself. Therefore he appears as he is in himself to be a sun above the angelic heavens. He himself as wisdom emanates from that sun in the form of light, and he himself as love emanates from that sun in the form of heat. That sun is not God himself. The divine love and wisdom surrounding him as they first go forth from him come to angels' view as a sun.

"The Absolute in that sun is the Human Being. It is *our Lord Jesus Christ*, including both the divine source and the divine-human manifestation. Since the Absolute, which is absolute love and absolute wisdom, was in him as his soul from the Father, therefore divine life or life in itself was in him. None of us is like this. The soul in us is not life; it is merely a vessel for receiving life.

"In fact, the Lord teaches this when he says, 'I am the way, the truth, and *the life*' (John 14:6); and in another passage, 'Just as the Father has *life* in himself, so he has also granted the Son to have *life* in himself' (John 5:26). 'Life in himself' is God."

They added that people who have any spiritual light at all can see from all this that the underlying divine reality, which is also the divine essence, cannot be shared among many, because it is united, uniform, absolute, and undivided. If anyone were to claim that the divine reality could be shared, further points that person made on the subject would contain obvious contradictions.

[6] Then the angels became aware that my thoughts included common Christian ideas of God: ideas of a trinity of persons in unity, and a unity of persons in the Trinity, and also of the Son of God's birth from eternity. At that point they said, "What are you thinking? Surely you are thinking those thoughts from an earthly light that is incompatible with our spiritual light. We are closing heaven to you and leaving unless you get rid of the ideas that go with that point of view."

So I said, "Please go deeper into my thinking. Perhaps you will see a compatibility."

They went deeper and saw that three persons to me meant three emanating divine activities: creating, redeeming, and regenerating, which are activities of the one only God. The birth of a Son of God from eternity to me meant his birth foreseen from eternity and carried out in time.

Then I explained that my earthly thoughts about the trinity and the unity of persons and about the eternally begotten Son of God were based on the church's statement of faith that was named after Athanasius. I added that the Athanasian Creed is accurate, provided that instead of the trinity of persons mentioned there one substitutes a trinity in one person—a trinity that exists uniquely within *the Lord Jesus Christ;* and provided that instead of the birth of a Son of God from eternity one substitutes the birth foreseen from eternity and carried out in time, because his human manifestation is openly referred to as *the Son of God.*

[7] The angels then said, "Good, good."

They asked me to pass on a statement from them: "Anyone who does not seek help from the absolute God of heaven and earth cannot come into heaven, because heaven is heaven as a result of the one only God. *The absolute God is Jesus Christ,* who is Jehovah the Lord, Creator from eternity, Redeemer in time, and Regenerator to eternity. He is the Father, the Son, and the Holy Spirit combined. This is the gospel that needs to be preached."

Afterward the heavenly light I had seen above the opening came back. It came down bit by bit and filled the inner reaches of my mind, enlightening my ideas of the unity and the trinity of God. Then I saw my former merely earthly ideas being separated out, just as husks are shaken off wheat tossed in a winnowing basket. I saw my old notions carried off as if by a wind to the north of heaven and scattered.

The third memorable occurrence taken from Revelation Unveiled. Since the Lord has allowed me to see amazing things in the heavens and below them, I have been commanded and am obligated to pass on what I have seen. **120**

I saw a magnificent palace that had a chapel in its center. In the middle of the chapel there was a golden table that had the Word on it. Two angels were standing next to the table. Around the table there were three rows of chairs. The chairs in the first row were covered in pure silk of a purple color, the chairs in the second row in pure silk of a sky blue color, and the chairs in the third row in white cloth. High above the table a canopy was suspended beneath the ceiling. It gleamed so brightly with precious stones that it created an effect like a glowing rainbow [that appears] when the sky begins to clear after a rain shower.

Suddenly members of the clergy appeared, occupying all the chairs. They were all wearing the robes of their priestly ministry.

To one side there was a cabinet with an angel guard standing nearby. Inside the cabinet there were shining pieces of clothing laid out in a beautiful array.

[2] It was *a council that had been called by the Lord.* I heard a voice from heaven that said, "*Discuss.*"

The participants said, "About what?"

"About *the Lord the Savior* and about *the Holy Spirit,*" the voice said.

When they began thinking about these topics they had no enlightenment, so they prayed. Then a light flowed down from heaven that first lit up the backs of their heads, then their temples, and finally their faces.

Then they began. They started where they had been told to, with the first topic, *the Lord the Savior.* The first issue to be discussed was, "*Who took on a human manifestation in the Virgin Mary?*"

An angel standing next to the table where the Word lay read to them the following words in Luke:

> The angel said to Mary, "Behold, you will conceive in your womb and bear a Son, and you will call his name *Jesus.* He will be great and will be called *the Son of the Highest.*" And Mary said to the angel, "How will this take place, since I have not had intercourse?" The angel replied and said to her, "*The Holy Spirit will descend upon you, and the power of the Highest will cover you;* therefore *the Holy One* that is born from you will be called *the Son of God.*" (Luke 1:31, 32, 34, 35)

Then the angel read Matthew 1:20–25; he raised his voice when he read verse 25. In addition, he read many other things from the Gospels, such as Matthew 3:17; 17:5; John 20:31; and other passages where the Lord in his human manifestation is referred to as *the Son of God,* and where from his human manifestation he calls Jehovah *his Father.* The angel also read from the Prophets where it is foretold that Jehovah himself is going to come into the world. Two of the latter passages were the following from Isaiah:

> It will be said on that day, "Behold, *this is our God;* we have waited for him to set us free. *This is Jehovah;* we have waited for him. Let us rejoice and be glad in his salvation." (Isaiah 25:9)

> A voice of someone in the wilderness crying out, "Prepare a pathway for *Jehovah;* make level in the desert a highway for *our God.* The glory of *Jehovah* will be revealed, and all flesh will see it together. Behold, *the Lord Jehovih is coming in strength.* Like a shepherd he will feed his flock." (Isaiah 40:3, 5, 10, 11)

[3] The angel said, "Jehovah himself came into the world and took on a human manifestation and by so doing redeemed and saved people; therefore in the Prophets Jehovah is called *the Savior* and *the Redeemer.*"

Then the angel read them the following passages:

> "*God* is only among you; and *there is no God except him.*" Surely you are a hidden *God, O God of Israel, the Savior.* (Isaiah 45:14, 15)

> Am not *I Jehovah? And there is no God other than me.* I am a just God, and *there is [no] Savior other than me.* (Isaiah 45:21, 22)

> *I am Jehovah, and there is no Savior other than me.* (Isaiah 43:11)

I am Jehovah your God. You are to acknowledge no God other than me. *There is no Savior other than me.* (Hosea 13:4)

. . . so that all flesh may know that I, *Jehovah, am your Savior, and your Redeemer.* (Isaiah 49:26; 60:16)

As for our Redeemer, Jehovah Sabaoth is his name. (Isaiah 47:4)

Their Redeemer is strong; Jehovah Sabaoth is his name. (Jeremiah 50:34)

. . . *Jehovah, my Rock and my Redeemer.* (Psalms 19:14)

Thus says *Jehovah your Redeemer,* the Holy One of Israel, "I am *Jehovah your God."* (Isaiah 43:14; 48:17; 49:7; 54:8)

You, Jehovah, are our Father; *our Redeemer* from everlasting is your name. (Isaiah 63:16)

Thus says *Jehovah your Redeemer:* "*I am Jehovah,* who makes all things, doing so alone, by myself." (Isaiah 44:24)

Thus says Jehovah the King of Israel, and *Israel's Redeemer, Jehovah Sabaoth:* "I am the First and the Last, and there is no God other than me." (Isaiah 44:6)

Jehovah Sabaoth is his name, and *your Redeemer,* the Holy One of Israel. *He will be called the God of the whole earth.* (Isaiah 54:5)

Behold, the days are coming when I will raise up for David a righteous branch who will rule as king. And this is his name: *Jehovah our Righteousness.* (Jeremiah 23:5, 6; 33:15–16)

On that day Jehovah will become king over all the earth. *On that day Jehovah will be one, and his name one.* (Zechariah 14:9)

[4] With the support of all these passages, the clergy sitting in the chairs unanimously stated that it was Jehovah himself who took on the human manifestation, and that he did so in order to redeem and save humankind.

At that point, though, we heard a voice from Roman Catholics who had hidden behind the altar. The voice said, "How could Jehovah the Father become human? He is the creator of the universe!"

One of the clergy sitting in the second row of chairs turned and said, "Who then was the human manifestation?"

The man who had been behind the altar before, but was now standing beside it, said, "*The Son from eternity.*"

He received this reply: "In your confession the eternally begotten Son is the same as the creator of the universe. What is a Son or a God who is eternally begotten? How could the divine essence, which is one indivisible thing, be separated? How could one part of it come down and not the whole essence at once?"

[5] *The second issue for discussion related to the Lord:* "Surely then the Father and he are one as the soul and the body are one."

They said that this would follow, because his soul was from the Father.

Then one of the clergy sitting in the third row of chairs read the following words from the statement of faith known as the Athanasian Creed: "Our Lord Jesus Christ, the Son of God, is God and a human being. Yet he is not two, but one Christ. Indeed, he is one altogether; he is *one person. Therefore as the soul and the body make one human being, so God and a human being is one Christ.*"

The reader said, "The creed that contains these words has been accepted by the entire Christian world including Roman Catholics."

The participants said, "What more do we need? God the Father and he are one as the soul and the body are one."

They added, "As this is so, we see that the Lord's human manifestation is divine because it is the human manifestation of Jehovah. We also see that we must seek help from the Lord's divine-human manifestation. Only in this way, not in any other, can we have access to the divine nature that is called the Father."

[6] The angel supported their conclusion with more passages from the Word, among which were the following in Isaiah:

> A Child has been born to us; a Son has been given to us. His name will be called Wonderful, Counselor, *God,* Hero, *Father of Eternity,* Prince of Peace. (Isaiah 9:6)

> Abraham did not know us and Israel did not acknowledge us. *You, Jehovah, are our Father; our Redeemer from everlasting is your name.* (Isaiah 63:16)

And in John,

> *Jesus said,* "Those who believe in me believe in the one who sent me; and those who *see me see the one* who *sent me.*" (John 12:44, 45)

Philip said to Jesus, "Show us the Father." Jesus said to him, "*Those who have seen me have seen the Father.* How then can you say, 'Show us the Father'? Do you not believe that *I am in the Father and the Father is in me? Believe me that I am in the Father and the Father is in me.*" (John 14:8, 9, 10, 11)

Jesus said, "*I and the Father are one.*" (John 10:30)

Also,

All things that the Father has are mine and all things that I have are the Father's. (John 16:15; 17:10)

And finally,

Jesus said, "*I am the way, the truth, and the life. No one comes to the Father except through me.*" (John 14:6)

When the participants had heard this they all said with one voice and one heart, "The Lord's human manifestation is divine. For us to gain access to the Father we have to go to his human manifestation, since this is how Jehovah God, who is the Lord from eternity, put himself in the world and made himself visible to human eyes. Through this he became accessible. Jehovah God also made himself visible and therefore accessible in a human form to the ancients; but back then he used an angel."

[7] The next discussion focused on *the Holy Spirit*. First there was a disclosure of the way many people picture *God the Father, the Son, and the Holy Spirit.* They picture God the Father sitting on high with the Son at his right hand. Both of them send out the Holy Spirit to enlighten and teach people.

Then a voice was heard out of heaven saying, "We do not support these mental images. Jehovah God is omnipresent, as everyone knows. If we know and acknowledge this, we also must acknowledge that Jehovah God is the one who enlightens and teaches us. There is no mediating God who is distinct from him as if they were two separate people, let alone a God who is distinct from two other gods. That earlier meaningless picture needs to be removed and this proper picture needs to be accepted. Then you will see this point clearly."

[8] Then we again heard a voice from the Roman Catholics. They had hidden behind the altar in the chapel. The voice said, "What then is *the Holy Spirit* mentioned in the Word by the Gospel writers and Paul, by

which so many learned clergy say they are led, especially in our denomination? Surely no one in the Christian world nowadays denies the existence of the Holy Spirit and its actions."

One of the clergy in the second row of chairs turned and said, "You are saying that the Holy Spirit is a person on its own and a god on its own; but what is a 'person' going out and emanating from a person if not an influence going out and emanating? A person cannot go out and emanate from another person through yet another, but an influence can. To put it another way, a god going out and emanating from a god is actually a divine influence going out and emanating. One god cannot go out and emanate from another through yet another, but a divine influence can. The divine essence is one indivisible thing. And since the divine essence or the underlying divine reality is God, therefore there is one indivisible God."

[9] After hearing that, the clergy sitting in the chairs unanimously concluded that the Holy Spirit is not a person on its own or a god on its own; it is the holy divine influence that goes out and emanates from the unique and omnipresent God, who is the Lord.

The angels who were standing by the golden table that held the Word responded to that by saying, "*Good!* Nowhere in the Old Covenant does it say that the prophets spoke the Word of the Holy Spirit. They spoke the Word of Jehovah the Lord. When the New Covenant speaks of the Holy Spirit, it means the divine influence that goes forth enlightening people, teaching them, bringing them to life, reforming them, and regenerating them."

[10] After that another issue related to *the Holy Spirit* came up: "From whom does the divine influence meant by the Holy Spirit emanate? Does it emanate from the divine nature, which is called the Father, or from the divine-human manifestation, which is called the Son?"

While they were discussing this a light shone down on them from heaven. In that light they saw that the holy divine influence meant by the Holy Spirit emanates from the divine nature in the Lord through his glorified human manifestation, which is the divine-human manifestation. It is comparable to the situation with human beings. Our actions emanate from our souls through our bodies.

An angel who was standing by the table supported this point with the following passages from the Word:

> The one whom the Father sent speaks the words of God; *God has not given him the spirit by measure.* The Father loves the Son and has given all things into his hand. (John 3:34, 35)

A shoot will go forth from the trunk of Jesse. *The spirit of Jehovah* will rest upon him, *the spirit of wisdom and intelligence, the spirit of counsel and strength.* (Isaiah 11:1, 2)

The spirit of Jehovah has been put upon him and is in him. (Isaiah 42:1; 59:19, 20; 61:1; Luke 4:18)

When *the Holy Spirit* comes, whom I will send to you from the Father . . . (John 15:26)

He will glorify me, because he will take *of what is mine* and declare it to you. All things that the Father has are mine. That is why I said that he will take *of what is mine* and declare it to you. (John 16:14, 15)

If I go away, I will send the Comforter to you. (John 16:7)

The Comforter is *the Holy Spirit.* (John 14:26)

There was not the Holy Spirit yet because Jesus was not yet glorified. (John 7:39)

After he was glorified, Jesus breathed on his disciples and said, *"Receive the Holy Spirit."* (John 20:22)

And in the Book of Revelation,

Who will not glorify your name, O Lord? For *you alone are holy.* (Revelation 15:4)

[11] The angel continued, "Since the Holy Spirit means the Lord's divine influence that results from his divine omnipresence, when he told his disciples about the Holy Spirit that he was going to send to them from God the Father he also said, 'I will not leave you orphans. *I am going away and coming [back] to you;* and on that day you will know that I am in my Father, and you are in me, and I am in you' (John 14:18, 20, 28). And just before he left the world he said, 'Behold, I am with you all the days, even to the close of the age' (Matthew 28:20)."

After reading these passages the angel said, "It is clear from these passages and many others in the Word that the divine influence called the Holy Spirit emanates from the divine nature in the Lord through his divine-human manifestation."

In response the clergy sitting in the chairs said, "This is *divine truth!*"

[12] At the end the participants produced the following declaration: "From the discussions in this council, we have come to see clearly and to

acknowledge as the sacred truth that the divine trinity exists in the Lord God the Savior Jesus Christ. The Trinity is made up of the divine nature as an origin called 'the Father,' the divine-human manifestation called 'the Son,' and the emanating divine influence called 'the Holy Spirit.' We proclaim then that '*all the fullness of divinity dwells physically in Jesus Christ*' (Colossians 2:9). Therefore there is one God in the church."

[13] After the events of this magnificent council came to an end, the participants stood up. The angel guarding the cabinet came over and brought shining clothing to each one of those who had been sitting in the chairs. The clothing was interwoven here and there with golden threads. The angel said, "Please accept these *wedding garments*."

The participants were led in glory to the new Christian heaven, which is going to be connected to the church of the Lord on earth, which is the New Jerusalem.

Zechariah 14:7, 8, 9

One day that is known to Jehovah *will not be day or night, because there will be light around the time of evening. On that day living waters will go forth from Jerusalem.* Jehovah *will become king over all the earth. On that day* Jehovah *will be one, and his name one.*

The End

Soul-Body Interaction

Believed to Occur

either by

A Physical Inflow

or by

A Spiritual Inflow

or by

A Preestablished Harmony

By Emanuel Swedenborg

Soul-Body Interaction

[Author's Introduction]

THERE have been three grand theories—hypotheses, actually—of the nature of the interaction between the soul and the body, meaning the way one affects the other and cooperates with it. The first of these is known as "physical inflow," the second "spiritual inflow," and the third "preestablished harmony."

The first, called *physical inflow,* is based on the way things seem to our senses and on the deceptive appearances that result, since it seems as though the objects of sight that affect our eyes flow into our thinking and make thoughts happen. In the same way, it seems as though the conversations that affect our ears flow into our minds and cause ideas to form there. We could say much the same of smell, taste, and touch as well. Because our sensory organs first receive the stimuli that impinge on them from the world, and because the mind seems both to think and to will things in response to those stimuli, the classical philosophers and Scholastics believed that an inflow from our sense impressions impinged on our soul. This led them to come up with the hypothesis that the inflow between the two was physical, or earthly, in nature.

[2] *The second view,* called *spiritual inflow* (some call it "occasional inflow"), is based on the laws of the divine design. It sees the soul as a spiritual substance and therefore something purer, primary, and inward; while the body is matter and is therefore coarser, secondary, and outward. In the divine design, what is purer flows into what is coarser, what is primary flows into what is secondary, and what is inward flows into what is outward. Therefore what is spiritual flows into what is material, and not the reverse. To be more specific, the part of our mind devoted to thinking flows into our eyesight in accordance with the state imposed on our

109

eyes by the objects we are seeing, and also imposes its own priorities on that state. In the same way, the part of our mind devoted to perception flows into our hearing in accordance with the state imposed on our ears by what is being said.

[3] *The third view,* called *preestablished harmony,* is based on plausible rational fallacies, because when the mind is producing an effect it does so in unison and simultaneously with the body. However, every deed starts out sequential and only later becomes simultaneous. Inflow is sequential, and harmony is simultaneous, as we can see when the mind thinks something and then says it or when it wills something and then does it. It is a rational fallacy, then, to insist that there is a simultaneous aspect yet deny that there is a [prior] sequential one.

These three are the only possible theories—there is no fourth. The soul activates the body, or the body activates the soul, or the two are constantly acting in unison.

2   Since spiritual inflow is based on the laws of the divine design, as just noted, it has been more widely acknowledged and accepted in the learned world than the other two theories. Every theory that is based on the divine design is true, and the truth, because of its inherent light, makes itself visible even in those shadowy realms of reason where hypotheses dwell.

There are three factors that cause the shadows around this particular hypothesis: ignorance of the nature of the soul, ignorance of the nature of what is spiritual, and ignorance of the nature of inflow. These three issues, then, need to be addressed before reason can see the actual truth. Hypothetical truth is not actual truth but a guess at the truth. It is like a painting on a wall seen by starlight at night—our minds can project one form or another onto it, depending on our imagination. The situation is different after dawn, though, when the sunlight shines on it and discloses to our sight not just its general outlines but its specific details. In the same way, truth emerges into the open from the shadows where hypotheses dwell when we recognize the reality and nature of what is spiritual relative to what is earthly; the reality and nature of the human soul; and the nature of what flows into the soul, then flows through it into the parts of the mind devoted to perception and thinking, and then through them into the body.

[2] However, no one can convey all this except someone whom the Lord has allowed to associate with angels in the spiritual world while still being

with people in this earthly world. Since this privilege has been granted to
me, I have been able to describe the reality and nature of these things. This
was done in my treatise *Marriage Love,* where there is a discussion of *what
is spiritual* in the account recorded in §§326–329, of *the human soul* in §315,
and of *inflow* in §380 and at greater length in §§415–422.

Surely everyone knows, or is at least capable of knowing, that the
goodness of love and the truth of faith flow into us from God, and that
they flow into our souls and are sensed in our minds, and flow from
our thoughts into our words and from our will into our actions.

[3] The following sequence of points, then, will show that inflow is
spiritual, and reveal its origin and derivation.

1. There are two worlds: a spiritual world where spirits and angels live,
   and an earthly world where we live.
2. The spiritual world came into being and is kept in existence from its
   sun, and the earthly world, from its sun.
3. The sun of the spiritual world is pure love from Jehovah God, who is
   at its center.
4. Warmth and light emanates from that sun; the essence of that emanating warmth is love, and the essence of the emanating light is wisdom.
5. Both spiritual warmth and spiritual light flow into us. The warmth
   flows into our will and gives rise there to a love for doing what is
   good, and the light flows into our understanding and gives rise [there]
   to the truth that leads to wisdom.
6. These two—spiritual warmth and spiritual light, or love and wisdom—
   flow together from God into the human soul, flow through our soul
   into our mind and its feelings and thoughts, and flow from there into
   our physical senses, speech, and actions.
7. The sun of our earthly world is nothing but fire, and is the means by
   which this earthly world came into being and is kept in existence.
8. This means that everything that emanates from the physical sun is in
   and of itself dead.
9. What is spiritual wears what is physical the way we wear clothes.
10. It is spiritual elements clothed in this way that enable us to live as
    rational and moral beings—that is, to live spiritually on this earthly
    level.
11. How receptive we are to this inflow depends on the state of love and
    wisdom within us.

12. Our understanding can be lifted into the light (that is, the wisdom) that angels enjoy to the extent that our rational ability has been cultivated; and our will can be elevated into the warmth, or love, [of heaven,] depending on how we live our lives. However, the love in our will becomes elevated only to the extent that we will and do what the wisdom in our understanding teaches us.

13. It is totally different for animals.

14. [Unknown until now,] there are three levels in the spiritual world and three in this earthly world, and these shape the way all inflow happens.

15. Purposes are on the first level, means on the second, and results on the third.

16. This shows us the nature of spiritual inflow, from its origin to its results.

Now I need to present brief explanations of these items.

I

There are two worlds: a spiritual world where spirits and angels live, and an earthly world where we live.

3 Up to the present time, the world—even the Christian world—has been oblivious to the fact that there is a spiritual world where spirits and angels live, quite distinct from the earthly world where we live. This is because no angel has come down and told us about it explicitly, and no one has gone up and seen it. To keep ignorance of that world and a consequent uncertainty about heaven and hell from deluding people so completely that they become materialistic atheists, the Lord has graciously opened the sight of my spirit, both raising it up into heaven and sending it down into hell to show me visibly what each realm is like.

[2] This has enabled me to see that there are two worlds and that they are distinct from each other. There is one where everything is spiritual and which is therefore called "the spiritual world," and one in which everything is earthly, and which is therefore called "the earthly world." I have been shown that spirits and angels live in their world and that we live in ours, and also that everyone crosses by death from our world into the other and lives there to eternity.

Knowledge of the existence of these two worlds is prerequisite if we are to trace inflow from its source, which is our present task. The spiritual world does in fact flow into the earthly world and animate it in detail both in humans and in animals. It is also what allows trees and plants to grow.

2

The spiritual world came into being and is kept in existence from its sun, and the earthly world, from its sun.

The reason there is one sun of the spiritual world and another sun of the earthly world is that these worlds are quite distinct from each other, and a world has its origin in a sun. A world in which everything is spiritual cannot arise from a sun that yields only earthly things, since this would be a physical inflow, which violates the basic design.

4

We can be assured that the world has arisen from its sun and not the reverse by the relationship between cause and effect, noting that in every respect our world is sustained by its sun, and the way it is sustained shows the way in which it arose. That is why we say that "enduring is a constant coming into being." We can see from this that if the sun were taken away, the world would collapse into chaos and then into nothingness.

[2] I can testify that the spiritual world has a different sun from the one in the earthly world because I have seen it. Like our sun, it looks fiery and about the same size. It is far away from angels, as our sun is from us, but does not rise or set. Rather, it stands still halfway between the zenith and the horizon, which gives angels a constant light and a constant springtime.

[3] Rationalists who are not aware of the spiritual world's sun may readily develop insane concepts of the creation of the universe. When they think deeply about that creation, all they can discern is that it comes from nature; and since the source of nature is the physical sun, they can think only that creation comes from the sun as its creator.

Further, people cannot grasp anything about spiritual inflow unless they also know where it comes from. All inflow comes from a sun, spiritual inflow from its sun and earthly inflow from its sun. Our inner sight, the sight of our minds, receives an inflow from the spiritual sun; while our outer sight, our physical sight, receives an inflow from the earthly sun. The two kinds of sight are coordinated in their activities the way the soul is coordinated with the body.

[4] We can see from this the blindness, darkness, and folly that people can fall into if they do not know anything about the spiritual world and its sun. There is *blindness* because the mind that relies in its logical operations wholly and only on what the eye can see is like a bat that flies erratically and sporadically toward towels on a clothesline at night. There is *darkness* because when our mental sight is subservient to what flows into the sight of our eyes it is deprived of any spiritual light and becomes like the eyesight of an owl; and there is *folly* because although we go right on thinking, we think about spiritual matters on the basis of earthly matters and not the reverse, which means that our thinking becomes deranged, stupid, and foolish.

3

The sun of the spiritual world is pure love from Jehovah God, who is at its center.

5   The only possible source of spiritual realities is love, and the only possible source of love is Jehovah God, who is love itself. This means that the spiritual world's sun, from which all spiritual realities issue as from their wellspring, is pure love emanating from Jehovah God, who is at its center. That sun is not God, but it is from God. It is a field emanating from himself that most closely surrounds him. It was by means of this sun that Jehovah God created the universe, meaning all the worlds taken together—as many as there are stars in the vast expanse of our sky.

[2] The reason creation was accomplished by means of this sun, which is pure love, and therefore by Jehovah God, is that love is the essential reality of life and wisdom is the resulting manifestation of life; and everything was created out of love, by means of wisdom. This is what the Gospel of John means when it says "The Word was with God, and the Word was God. All things were made through him, nothing that was made came about without him, and the world was made through him" (John 1:1, 3, 10). "The Word" here is divine truth and therefore also divine wisdom. So too, in John 1:9 the Word is called the light that enlightens everyone, the way divine wisdom does by means of divine truth.

[3] If people trace the origin of the worlds to any source other than divine love by means of divine wisdom, they are hallucinating like the

mentally ill who see ghosts as real people, apparitions as lights, and figments of their own imagination as images of reality. The created universe is actually a coherent work, from love by means of wisdom. If you are able to explore the connections in the divine design from beginning to end, you will certainly see this for yourself.

[4] Just as God is one, the spiritual sun is one as well, since we cannot attribute spatial extension to the spiritual things that are derived from such a sun. Nonspatial essence and manifestation is everywhere in space without being limited by space, so divine love is present from the beginning of the universe to all its remotest boundaries. Reason can see, at least from a distance, that Divinity fills everything and by so doing maintains everything in its created state. Reason can even see this close at hand if it knows what love is really like, how love works with wisdom to identify purposes, how love flows into wisdom to establish means, and how love operates through wisdom to achieve results.

4

Warmth and light emanates from that sun; the essence of that emanating warmth is love, and the essence of the emanating light is wisdom.

It is common knowledge that in the Word, and therefore in typical sermons of the clergy, divine love is expressed as fire. For example, there are prayers that heavenly fire may fill our hearts and kindle a holy longing to worship God. This is because fire corresponds to love and therefore symbolizes it. This is why Jehovah God appeared to Moses as fire in a burning bush [Exodus 3:2] and to the Israelites as fire on Mount Sinai. It is the reason for the biblical command to keep a fire burning constantly on the altar [Leviticus 6:13] and to light the lamps on the lampstand in the tabernacle every evening [Exodus 30:8]. This was because that fire meant love.

[2] If we consider the effects love has on us, it is obvious that we gain warmth from this fire. We become kindled, heated, and inflamed as our love is intensified into zeal or into the blaze of anger. The warmth of our blood, our own vital warmth (and that of animals in general), comes solely from the love that constitutes our life. Hellfire is nothing but love that is opposite to heavenly love. This, then, is why angels see divine love as the sun in their world, a sun that as already noted [§4] is fiery like our own sun. It is why angels are warmed to the extent that they are receptive to love from Jehovah God through that sun.

[3] It follows from this that the essence of the light in heaven is wisdom. Love and wisdom are inseparable, like the underlying reality and its manifestation. Love in fact manifests itself through wisdom and in accord with wisdom, much as in our world the warmth of spring joins with light and causes plants to sprout and eventually to bear fruit. Then too, everyone knows that spiritual warmth is love and spiritual light is wisdom: when we are loving we are warm, and when we are wise our minds are enlightened.

[4] I have seen this spiritual light quite often. It is far clearer and more brilliant than earthly light; it is like clarity itself and brilliance itself. It looks like bright, sparkling snow, like the Lord's clothing when he was transfigured (Mark 9:3; Luke 9:29). Because light is wisdom, the Lord calls himself the light that enlightens everyone (John 1:9) and says elsewhere that he is light itself (John 3:19, 8:12, 12:35, 36, 46), that is, that he is divine truth itself, the truth that is the Word, and therefore is wisdom itself.

[5] Some people believe that earthly, rational enlightenment comes from the light of our world, but it actually comes from the sunlight in the spiritual world. The sight of our mind flows into our eyesight, so spiritual rays of light do the same. It does not happen the other way around; if it did, that would be a physical inflow and not a spiritual inflow.

5

Both spiritual warmth and spiritual light flow into us. The warmth flows into our will and gives rise there to a love for doing what is good, and the light flows into our understanding and gives rise there to the truth that leads to wisdom.

7 It is recognized that absolutely everything goes back to what is good and what is true, and that there is nothing whatever that does not have something in it that is related to these two realities. That is why there are two vessels of life in us, a vessel for what is good, called our will, and a vessel for what is true, called our understanding. Since what is good has to do with love and what is true has to do with wisdom, our will is a vessel for love and our understanding is a vessel for wisdom.

The reason what is good has to do with love is that we will what we love, and when we do what we love we call it a good thing. The reason what is true has to do with wisdom is that all wisdom is based on truths. In fact, when wise people think of doing something good, that thought is a truth; and it becomes something good when they will it and do it.

[2] If we do not make the proper distinction between these two vessels of life, the will and the understanding, and construct a clear idea of their nature, we labor in vain to understand spiritual inflow, since there is one type of flow into our will and another type into our understanding. Into our will flows a love for doing what is good and into our understanding flows the truth that leads to wisdom. Both of these come to us directly from Jehovah God, by means of the sun that surrounds him, and both of them also come to us indirectly through the angelic heaven.

These two vessels, our will and our understanding, are as distinct from each other as warmth and light, since our will receives heaven's warmth, which in its essence is love, and our understanding receives heaven's light, which in its essence is wisdom, as noted above.

[3] From the human mind there is one type of flow into speech and another into deeds. The flow into speech comes from our will through our understanding, while the one into deeds comes from our understanding through our will. If people recognize only the flow into the understanding and not at the same time the flow into the will and draw their rational conclusions from this, they are like people who have only one eye and see things from one side only and not from the other. Or they are like handicapped people who twist around because they have only one hand to work with, or lame people who hop along on one foot and a cane.

These few words clarify that spiritual warmth flows into our will and gives rise to a love for doing what is good and that spiritual light flows into our understanding and gives rise to the truth that leads to wisdom.

6

These two—spiritual warmth and spiritual light, or love and wisdom— flow together from God into the human soul, flow through our soul into our mind and its feelings and thoughts, and flow from there into our physical senses, speech, and actions.

The spiritual inflow proposed by polished intellects of the past flows from the soul into the body. They did not, however, recognize any inflow into

8

the soul or through the soul into the body. Nevertheless it is known that all love for doing what is good and all truth that leads to wisdom flow into us from the Lord; that no trace of love or wisdom comes from us; and that whatever flows in from the Lord flows first of all into the soul, then through the soul into the rational mind, and through this into the constituent parts of the body. If we investigate spiritual inflow under any other framework, it is like damming up the flow of a spring and still expecting a constant stream of water from it, or positing the origin of a tree in its roots rather than its seed, or studying phenomena that are actually secondary without considering their source.

[2] The soul is not life in and of itself. It is a vessel for life from God, who *is* life in and of itself; and all inflow of life is from God. This is the meaning of the statement that "Jehovah God breathed into the human's nostrils the breath of lives, and the human was made into a living soul" (Genesis 2:7). "Breathing the breath of lives into the nostrils" means instilling a perception of what is good and true. Then too, the Lord says of himself, "Just as the Father has life in himself, so he has also granted the Son to have life in himself" (John 5:26). "Life in himself" is God, and the life of the soul is life that is flowing in from God.

[3] Given the fact, then, that all inflow is an inflow of life, that it works through its recipient vessels, and that the central or first vessel in us is our soul, it follows that if we are to understand inflow properly we must start with God and not at some halfway point. If we were to do the latter, our concept of inflow would be like a carriage without wheels or a ship without sails. That is why earlier in this work there was a discussion of the spiritual world's sun, which has Jehovah God at its center (§5), and of the inflow of love and wisdom—of life, therefore—from that source (§§6–7).

[4] The reason life from God flows into us through our souls into our minds (that is, into our feelings and thoughts) and flows from these into our physical senses, speech, and actions is that the above are the vessels of life in sequential order. The mind is subject to the soul and the body is subject to the mind. The mind has two kinds of life, one belonging to the will and the other to the understanding. The life in our will is the goodness of love, and its offshoots are called feelings. The life in our understanding is the truth that leads to wisdom, and its offshoots are called thoughts. Our mind is alive as a result of our feelings and thoughts. However, the life in our body is its senses, words, and actions. It follows

from the sequence in which things occur that these come from the soul through the mind. Just on the basis of this sequence, the wise see all this clearly without having to conduct further research.

[5] Since the human soul is a higher, spiritual substance, it receives an inflow directly from God. The human mind, though, being a lower spiritual substance, receives an inflow from God indirectly through the spiritual world; while the body, being made of the earthly substances we refer to as matter, receives an inflow from God indirectly through the earthly world.

We will see below [§14] that a love for doing what is good and the truth that leads to wisdom flow into our souls together—that is, absolutely united—but that we separate them as they proceed. They become rejoined only in people who allow themselves to be led by the Lord.

7

The sun of our earthly world is nothing but fire, and is the means by which this earthly world came into being and is kept in existence.

Nature and its world—meaning the atmospheres, the bodies we call planets, including the globe of lands and seas that is our home and everything that adorns its surface year after year—are sustained by the sun that is at their center and is able to be present everywhere by means of its rays of light and its tempered heat. This is something everyone knows with complete confidence, from personal observation and knowledge based on sensory experience, as well as from written information about what makes our world habitable. Since the sun is how everything is constantly sustained, reason can with complete confidence conclude that it is also how everything came into being, since constant being is a constant coming *into* being in the same manner in which it originally came about. It follows that our earthly world was created by Jehovah God through the agency of the physical sun.

[2] I have already explained that there is a spiritual realm and a physical realm that are clearly distinct from each other [§3]; and that the origin and support of spiritual realities is a sun that is pure love, and has the Creator and Maintainer of the universe, Jehovah God, at its center [§5].

This means that the origin and support of the earthly realm is a sun that is nothing but fire. This latter sun comes from the former, and both come from God. This follows as a matter of course, just as what is posterior comes from what is prior, and what is prior comes from the First.

[3] As for the sun that serves the physical realm and all the worlds in it, all the evidence it provides shows convincingly that it is pure fire. For example, when its rays are focused on a point by a lens, the result is an intense burning and even open flame; the nature of its heat is like that of ordinary fire; the levels of its warmth depend on its angle of incidence, providing us with our different climates and the four seasons of the year; besides many other examples. Our reason can use this evidence acquired through our physical senses to prove that the sun of our earthly world is nothing but fire, and that it is fire in its essential purity.

[4] If we have no idea that spiritual realities originate in their own sun, if we know only that earthly realities originate in their own sun, then we will almost inevitably confuse what is spiritual with what is physical. Rational thinking based on sensory illusions will lead us to believe that what is spiritual is nothing more than something relatively pure on the physical level, and that wisdom and love well up from these purer physical substances when they are stimulated by light and warmth. If nature is all we see with our eyes and sense with our nostrils and breathe with our lungs, then we attribute everything to it, even our own rational processes; and we soak up materialism the way a sponge soaks up water. If we do this, though, we are like carriage drivers who harness teams of horses to the back of the carriage rather than the front. [5] It is different if we draw a distinction between what is spiritual and what is earthly and see the latter as dependent on the former. Then we understand that the inflow of the soul into the body is spiritual. We understand that our earthly bodies serve our souls as vehicles and means so that they—our souls—can make things happen in this earthly world.

If you reach other conclusions, you are like a lobster moving backward by means of its tail, while its eyes are trained on where it has already been; and your rational sight is like that of an Argus seeing only with the eyes in the back of his head, while the eyes in front are asleep. Yet people like this think of themselves as being as clear-sighted as Argus when they reason. They say, "Can anyone fail to see that the universe comes from nature? What is God, then, but the deepest level of nature?" They say other irrational things as well, and take more pride in their thoughts than wise people do in thoughts that are actually rational.

8

This means that everything that emanates from the physical sun is in and of itself dead.

If at this point we raise the reasoning of our minds a little above our physical senses, can we fail to see that love is intrinsically alive and that what appears to be its fire is actually its life, and that on the other hand ordinary fire is intrinsically dead by comparison? This means that the sun of the spiritual world, being pure love, is alive, and that the sun of this earthly world, being pure fire, is dead. The same holds true for everything that emanates and arises from each.

[2] There are two things that produce all the effects in the universe: *life* and *nature*. If life is within nature and activates it to produce these effects, this accords with the divine design. The other view is that nature is what lies within and causes life to become active. This is held by people who put nature above and within life, even though it is intrinsically dead. As a result, they indulge in nothing but sensual pleasures and lusts of the flesh, and attach no importance whatever to pursuing spirituality in their souls or true rationality in their minds. Because they have turned everything upside down like this, they are called "the dead." [3] Theirs is the view held by all the materialistic atheists in the world and all the satans in hell. In the Word as well they are called "the dead": see in Psalms, for example, "They attached themselves to the Baal of Peor and ate the sacrifices of *the dead*" (Psalms 106:28); "The enemy is pursuing my soul; he makes me sit in darkness like *the dead* of the world" (Psalms 143:3); and "To hear the groaning of the prisoner and to open [a door] for *the children of death*" (Psalms 102:20); and in the Book of Revelation, "I know your works, that you have a name that you are alive, but you are *dead*. Be watchful, and strengthen the things that remain but are *about to die*" (Revelation 3:1, 2).

[4] They are called dead because damnation is spiritual death, and damnation is what awaits people who believe that life comes from nature and that nature's light is therefore the light of life. By doing so they conceal, stifle, and snuff out any concept of God, heaven, and eternal life. This makes them like owls that see light in darkness and darkness in light—that is, see false things as true and evil things as good. Then too, since evil pleasures are their heart's delight, they are not unlike birds and

animals that devour carrion as delicacies and experience the stenches of tombs as perfumes.

In addition, these people do not recognize any inflow other than a physical or earthly one. If they argue in favor of a spiritual inflow, this is not their own idea but something repeated from the mouth of a teacher.

9

What is spiritual wears what is physical the way we wear clothes.

11 It is widely recognized that every event involves both an active and a passive element, and that nothing happens if there is only an active element or only a passive one. The same holds true for what is spiritual and what is physical, because what is spiritual is a force that is living and active and what is physical is a force that is dead and passive. It follows then that anything that has come into being in our subsolar world and continues to exist at every moment comes from what is spiritual by means of what is physical. This is true not only of members of the animal kingdom but of members of the plant kingdom as well.

[2] A similar, widely recognized concept is that everything that happens has a principal and an instrumental component to it, and that when the event occurs these two components seem to be one, even though they are distinguishable as two. Therefore it is among the canons of received wisdom that a principal cause and an instrumental cause that are working together constitute a single cause. The same is true of what is spiritual and what is physical. The reason the two appear to be one when an event takes place is that the spiritual component lies within the physical component like a fiber within a muscle or blood within its arteries, or like thought within speech and feeling within tones of voice. In this way the spiritual component makes itself felt through the physical component. From this we can see, at least in a veiled way, that what is spiritual wears what is physical the way we wear clothes.

[3] The reason for comparing the bodily organism that the soul wears to a piece of clothing is that the body clothes the soul, and then the soul takes the body off and sheds it like a snake's skin when it crosses by death from the earthly world into its spiritual world. Then too, the body grows old like a piece of clothing, but the soul does not. This is because the soul is a spiritual substance and has nothing in common with the changes we

see in nature that progress from start to finish and end when their cycle is complete.

[4] If we do not consider the body to be a garment or covering for the soul, intrinsically dead and only adapted to receive the living energies that flow through the soul from God, all we can do is decide on the basis of our illusions that the soul lives on its own and the body lives on its own and that there is a *preestablished harmony* between the life within each. Or we may decide that the life within the soul flows into the life within the body or the life within the body flows into the life within the soul, and therefore envision either a *spiritual* or a *physical inflow* between the life within each. However, the truth proclaimed by all creation is that what is secondary does not act on its own but from what is prior to it—that is, its source. This too, then, does not act on its own but from something still prior, so that nothing happens except from a First that acts on its own, therefore from God. Further, there is only one life, and that life cannot be created; but it is in every way capable of flowing into forms organized and designed to receive it. Everything in the universe, great or small, is a form like this.

[5] Many people believe that the soul is life, and that since the soul is what gives us life, we are the source of our own life and live on our own, not from any inflow of life from God. If that is what we believe, we cannot help but weave a Gordian knot of illusions and entangle all the judgments of our minds in it. This leads to sheer insanity in spiritual matters. Or we construct a labyrinth from which our minds can never escape by following any thread of reason and retracing our steps. In fact, we actively lower ourselves, as if into underground caves where we live in eternal darkness. [6] This occurs because the resulting illusions are beyond number, and some of them are appalling. We might believe, for example, that God infuses and transcribes himself into us so that each of us becomes a kind of demigod with independent life. This would mean that we did what is good and were wise from our own resources and in the same vein that we ourselves possessed faith and charity and therefore produced them out of our own storehouse rather than receiving them from God.

There are other grotesque notions as well, like those held by the people in hell who during their earthly lives believed that nature was alive or that its activity caused life. When they look at heaven, they see its light as utter darkness.

[7] I once heard a voice from heaven saying that if the slightest spark of our life belonged to us and did not belong to God within us, there

would be no heaven and nothing in its place and therefore no church on earth and no eternal life. (There is more along these lines in the account in *Marriage Love* 132–136.)

10

It is spiritual elements clothed in this way that enable us to live as rational and moral beings—that is, to live spiritually on this earthly level.

12 The principle just established—that the soul wears the body the way we wear clothes—leads to the conclusion that the soul flows into the human mind and through it into the body, bringing with it the life that it is constantly receiving from the Lord. It therefore transfers life into the body by these means; and there, through the tightest of connections, it makes the body seem to be alive. This principle, along with the evidence of a thousand experiences, shows that what enables us to speak rationally and act morally is a spiritual element that is united to the physical, like a living force united to a dead one. [2] It does seem as though our tongue and lips talk because they have a life of their own and that our arms and hands move for the same reason. However, it is actually our thinking, which is essentially spiritual, that is speaking and our will, which is likewise spiritual, that stirs us to action. Thinking and willing operate through organs that are thoroughly physical because what they are made of comes from the material world. The truth of this becomes as clear as day when we pay attention to the following: if we remove our thinking from what we are saying, our mouth is instantly silenced, and if we remove our will from our actions, our hands are instantly stilled.

[3] As for this uniting of spiritual and earthly realities and the consequent appearance that there is life in material things, we could compare it to fine wine in a clean sponge or the sweet liquid in a grape or the delicious juice in an apple or the fragrant aroma in cinnamon. All the enclosing fibers are materials that have no taste or fragrance of their own; the taste or fragrance is supplied only by the fluid elements that are in and among them. So if you press out those fluids, the fibers themselves are lifeless shreds. The same holds true of the organs of the body if we take away their life.

[4] It is spiritual qualities united to our earthly ones that make our rationality possible, as we can see from the analytical abilities present in

our thinking. From our capacity for decency of action and propriety of behavior we can see that the same applies to our morality as well. We have these capacities because of our ability to receive an inflow from the Lord through the angelic heaven, which is the home where wisdom and love and therefore rationality and morality live. These examples let us see that we have the ability to live spiritually on this earthly level because what is spiritual and what is earthly are united within us.

After death it is much the same, though not exactly so, because then our soul is clothed with a substantial body, whereas it was clothed with a material body in this world.

[5] Many people believe that since the perceptions and thoughts of our minds are spiritual, they flow in as they are, without going through organized structures. People who dream up such things have not seen the insides of the head, where perceptions and thoughts occur in their primary forms. For example, they have not seen that there are brains there, intricately woven of gray matter and medullary matter, that there are little glands, recesses, and partitions, all enclosed in meninges and membranes, and that our thinking and willing are either sound or insane depending on the healthy or disordered state of all these elements. Likewise, we are rational and moral according to the organic shape of our mind. Without forms structured for the reception of spiritual light, our rational sight, the sight of our intellect, would have no attributes. It would be like physical sight without eyes. And so on.

II

How receptive we are to this inflow depends on the state of love and wisdom within us.

I have already explained that we are not life but organs receptive of life, **13** that love united to wisdom is life, and that God is love itself and wisdom itself and therefore life itself [§§5, 8, 10, 11]. It then follows that we are images of God or receptors of life from God to the extent that we love wisdom, or hold wisdom in the embrace of love within ourselves. Conversely, to the extent that we engage in the opposite love and therefore in madness, we receive our life not from God but from hell, a life that is called death.

[2] By themselves love and wisdom do not constitute life, although they are the realities that lie behind it; it is the delights that accompany love and the pleasures that accompany wisdom, which are feelings, that constitute life. The underlying reality of life manifests itself by means of these feelings. The inflow of life from God brings with it these delights and pleasures the way light and warmth flow in and affect our minds in spring. Light and warmth flow into every kind of bird and beast as well and even into plants, which then sprout and flourish. This is because the delights of love and the pleasures of wisdom open our spirits and prepare them to be receptive, the way joy and happiness relax our faces and ready them for the inflow of the soul's good cheer.

[3] People moved by love for wisdom are like the Garden of Eden with its two trees, one of life and the other of the knowledge of good and evil [Genesis 2:9]. The tree of life is when we believe that love and wisdom come from the Lord; the tree of the knowledge of good and evil is when we believe that these qualities come from ourselves. In the latter case, we are insane, and yet believe that we are as wise as God. In the former case we are truly wise, and believe that no one is wise except God and that people are wise to the extent that they believe this—and even wiser to the extent that they feel they want it to be this way. (There is more on this subject in the account in *Marriage Love* 132–136.)

[4] In support of this, let me add a secret from heaven. All the angels of heaven turn their foreheads toward the Lord as the sun, and all the angels of hell turn the backs of their heads toward him. These latter are receptive to an inflow into the feelings that belong to their will—feelings that are basically cravings—and constrain their understanding to go along. The former are receptive to an inflow into the feelings that belong to their understanding and constrain their will to go along. As a result, these enjoy wisdom, while the others are deranged.

Our understanding resides in the cerebrum, which is behind the forehead, while our will resides in the cerebellum, which is in the back of the head. [5] Everyone knows that people who are crazed by false notions go along with the cravings associated with their type of evil and support them with reasons drawn from their understanding, whereas people who are wise see on the basis of truths the quality of the cravings in their will and hold them in check. The wise do this because they turn their faces toward God. That is, they put their trust in God and not in themselves. On the other hand, the deranged turn their faces away from God. That is, they put their trust in themselves and not in God. Trusting in ourselves is believing that we love and are wise on our own, and not from God. This is what "eating from the tree of the knowledge of good and evil" [Genesis 2:17; 3:3, 6] means. On the other hand, trusting in God is believing that we love and are wise from God and not on our own; and this is eating from the tree of life (Revelation 2:7).

[6] We may gather from all this (though only dimly, as if by moonlight at night) that how receptive we are to the inflow of life from God depends on our state of love and wisdom.

We may further illustrate this inflow by the inflow of light and warmth into plants. They bloom and bear fruit depending on the way the fibers that form them are woven together and therefore depending on their receptiveness. We may also illustrate it by the way light flows into precious stones, which turn the light into different colors depending on the positioning of their component parts and therefore again on their receptiveness. Or we could mention prisms and raindrops that make rainbows depending on the angles of incidence and refraction, and therefore on the way they receive the light. Human minds react similarly to the spiritual light that emanates from the Lord as the sun; it is constantly flowing in, but we receive it in different ways.

12

Our understanding can be lifted into the light (that is, the wisdom) that angels enjoy to the extent that our rational ability has been cultivated; and our will can be elevated into the warmth, or love, of heaven, depending on how we live our lives. However, the love in our will becomes elevated only to the extent that we will and do what the wisdom in our understanding teaches us.

The human mind means the two abilities called the understanding and the will. The understanding is a vessel for heaven's light, whose essence is wisdom, and the will is a vessel for heaven's warmth, whose essence is love, as already noted [§7]. These two energies, wisdom and love, emanate from the Lord as the sun and flow into heaven both universally and individually, giving angels their wisdom and love; and they also flow into this world both universally and individually, giving us our wisdom and love.

[2] However, while these two energies emanate from the Lord united and flow united into the souls of angels and people on earth, they are not received by our minds as one thing. The light that builds the understanding is received in us first; the love that builds the will is received only little by little. The reason for this arrangement is that we all need to be created anew, or reformed, and this is done by means of our understanding. From earliest childhood we gain knowledge of what is true and good, knowledge that teaches us how to live rightly, how to will and act rightly. In this way, our will is shaped by our understanding.

[3] This is why we have been gifted with the ability to lift our understanding almost into the light that surrounds heaven's angels, so that we can see what we ought to will and therefore do in order to be successful in this world, for the time being, and blessed after death, to eternity. We become successful and blessed if we acquire wisdom and keep our will subjected to it. We become unsuccessful and unhappy if we keep our understanding subjected to our will. This is because from our birth our will tends toward evil and even inclines to heinous acts; so if it is not held in check by our understanding it will plunge into unspeakable crimes. Its innate savagery will lead us, purely for self-centered reasons, to butcher and annihilate everyone who does not support and indulge us.

[4] Further, if our understanding were incapable of being separately improved and our will could not be improved by means of it, we would be beasts, not human beings. If it were not for this separation and the raising of our understanding to a higher level than our will, we would not be able to think or express thoughts in speech. We could only make noises to express our feelings. We would not be able to act rationally, either, only instinctively. Least of all would we be able to recognize what comes from God and thereby come to know God and be joined to God and live forever.

We seem to think and will autonomously, and this apparent autonomy allows us to reciprocate and be joined [to God]. This joining would be impossible without mutuality, just as what is passive cannot be joined to what is active without some ability to react to it. God alone acts, and we let ourselves be activated and react just as though we were autonomous, though on a deeper level this ability too comes from God.

[5] Once this is properly understood, we can see what the love in our will is like if it has been elevated by means of our understanding and what it is like if it has not—in short, what it is to be human.

Let me use some analogies to illustrate what we are like if our will has not been elevated by means of our understanding. We are like an eagle that soars high overhead, but at the first sight of prey below that appeals to its appetite—prey like hens or cygnets or even lambs—it plunges down and devours them. We are also like an adulterer who keeps a prostitute hidden in his basement; he goes back and forth to the top level of the house and there says wise things to his visitors about chastity, but then periodically breaks away from the group to go down and satisfy his lust with the prostitute. [6] We are also like a thief on a tower who pretends to be keeping guard there, but the moment he sees something he wants, he races down and steals it. We can also be compared to swamp flies that fly in a column above the head of a galloping horse, but plunge back down into the swamp when the horse comes to a stop.

This is what we are like when our will, or love, has not been elevated by means of our understanding. It remains down at the level of the feet, sunk in unclean earthly things and sense-centered lusts.

It is completely different for us if we have used our understanding to tame the seductive urges of the cravings in our will. Then our understanding enters into a marriage covenant with our will, our wisdom with our love, and together on high they share a life of delight.

13

It is totally different for animals.

People who base their judgments solely on the way things seem to their physical senses wind up believing that animals have a will and an understanding just the way we do, so that the only difference is that we can talk and therefore articulate the things we are thinking and desiring while animals can only make noises about them. Animals, though, do not have a will and an understanding. All they have is something that parallels these abilities, something scholars call "analogs."

[2] The reason we are human is that our understanding can be raised above the desires of our will, can then see and identify them from a higher

perspective, and can even regulate them. Animals are animals because their desires impel them to do what they do. This means that we are human because our will is subject to our understanding, while animals are animals because their understanding is subject to their will. This leads to the conclusion that our understanding is alive and is therefore truly an understanding, since it receives the inflowing light from heaven, takes hold of it and feels it to be its own, and uses it to think analytically in all kinds of ways with every appearance of independence; our will, since it receives heaven's inflowing love and acts on it in apparent independence, is alive and is truly a will. This is not the case with animals.

[3] As a result, people who base their thinking on the lusts of their will are compared to animals and in the spiritual world even look like animals from a distance. They act like animals as well, with the sole difference that they could act differently if they wanted to. People who control the lusts of their will by means of their understanding, though, and therefore behave rationally and wisely, look human in the spiritual world, and are angels of heaven.

[4] In short, the will and the understanding in animals are always inseparable; and since the will is by nature blind, being attuned to warmth and not light, it blinds their understanding as well. So animals do not know or comprehend what they are doing. Still, they do act; but their doing so is the result of an inflow from the spiritual world. This kind of behavior is instinctive.

[5] Some people believe that animals' actions are the result of thoughts they have in their understanding, but there is no truth whatever in this. They are impelled to action simply by an earthly love that is in them by creation, supported by their physical senses. The only reason we humans are able to think and talk is that our understanding can be separated from our will and raised up into the light of heaven, since it is our understanding that thinks and our thinking that speaks.

[6] Animals behave according to laws of the design written on their nature, and some of them, unlike many people, seem to behave morally and rationally. This is because their understanding is blindly obedient to their will, so they have not been able to corrupt it by perverted rationalizations the way we have.

Please note, however, that in the preceding discussion the "will" and "understanding" of animals actually means the likeness and analog of these faculties in them. The analogs are given these names because of how they seem.

[7] We may compare the life of animals to that of sleepwalkers, who walk around and do things on the basis of their will while their understanding is dormant. Or it is like blind people who are led along the road by a dog, or like cognitively impaired people who perform their work according to standards by sheer habit formed through repetition. Or we might compare the life of animals to that of people who suffer from amnesia and have lost their ability to function mentally as a result: they still know, or can learn, how to clothe themselves, eat good food, make love, leave home on a walk and find their way back again, driven by what they want and what feels good, despite the fact that they have no thoughts and therefore cannot talk.

[8] This shows how deluded people are if they believe that animals enjoy rationality and differ from humans only in outer shape and in their inability to articulate the rational processes hidden within them. These illusions lead many to conclude that if we live after death, so do animals, or conversely that if animals do not live after death, neither do we. These and many other fictions are the result of not knowing about the will and the understanding, or about the levels by which our minds, so to speak, climb the ladder to heaven.

14

Unknown until now, there are three levels in the spiritual world and three in this earthly world, and these shape the way all inflow happens.

Inquiry into causes from their effects leads to the discovery that there are two different kinds of levels, one kind that deals with prior versus subsequent, and one kind that deals with greater versus lesser. The ones that distinguish prior from subsequent are to be called *vertical* or *distinct levels*, while the ones that distinguish greater from lesser are to be called *horizontal* or *gradient levels*. [2] Examples of vertical or distinct levels may be found in the way one thing is generated by or composed of another—a nerve, for instance, is made up of fibers, and each fiber is made of fibrils; or every type of wood, stone, and metal is made of component elements, and each element is made of particles. In contrast, examples of horizontal or gradient levels are things on the same vertical level that lie along a range of greater or lesser length, width, height, or depth—such as larger or smaller volumes of water, air, or ether, for instance, or massive versus miniscule amounts of wood, stone, or metal.

16

[3] Everything great and small in the spiritual and physical worlds is characterized by both kinds of levels. The whole animal kingdom in this world is arranged in these levels overall and in detail, and so are the whole plant kingdom, the whole mineral kingdom, and even the span of atmospheres from the sun down to the earth.

[4] This means that in the spiritual world as well as in the physical world there are three atmospheres on distinct vertical levels, since there is a sun in each world. However, the atmospheres of the spiritual world are substantial by virtue of their origin; the atmospheres of the physical world are material in origin. Further, since the atmospheres come down from their origins by these levels, and since they are the vessels and, so to speak, the vehicles that transport light and warmth, it follows that there are three levels of light and warmth; and since the essence of the light in the spiritual world is wisdom and the essence of the warmth there is love, as explained in the appropriate section above [§6], it also follows that there are three levels of wisdom and three levels of love, and therefore three levels of life. The levels are characterized by the things that pass through them.

[5] As a result, there are three angelic heavens: a highest heaven, also called the third heaven, where angels of the highest level live; a middle heaven, also called the second heaven, where angels of the intermediate level live; and a lowest heaven, also called the first heaven, where angels of the lowest level live. These heavens are differentiated according to their levels of wisdom and love. Those in the lowest heaven are engaged in a love of knowing about what is true and good, those in the middle heaven are engaged in a love of understanding these matters, and those in the highest heaven are engaged in a love of being wise, which is a love of living according to what they know and understand.

[6] Because the angelic heaven is differentiated into three levels, the human mind, being an image of heaven or a heaven in miniature, is differentiated into three levels as well. This is why we can become angels of one or another of the three heavens; and this happens according to our acceptance of wisdom and love from the Lord. We become angels of the lowest heaven if we accept only a love of knowing about what is true and good, angels of the middle heaven if we accept a love of understanding these matters, and angels of the third heaven if we accept a love of being wise, that is, of living by them. On the division of the human mind into three areas matching the heavens, see the account included in *Marriage Love* 270.

We can see from all this that the spiritual inflow toward us and into us from the Lord comes down through these three levels, and that it is accepted by us according to the level of wisdom and love in which we are engaged.

[7] Familiarity with these levels is particularly useful nowadays because so many people, not knowing about them, are fixated on the lowest level, where our physical senses are. Being stuck in an ignorance that is a darkness in their understanding, they cannot rise into the spiritual light that is above them. As a result, materialism barges in of its own accord the moment they try to make serious inquiries into anything about the soul, the human mind, or its rational functions, and is even more intrusive if they inquire into heaven or life after death. They become like the people who stand outdoors, telescopes in hand, scanning the skies and uttering meaningless prophecies, or like the people who respond to every object they see and everything they hear by chattering on and on and arguing about it without a trace of rationality or understanding. Or they are like butchers who think they know all about anatomy because they have examined the outsides but not the insides of the organs of cattle and sheep.

[8] The truth of the matter is that unless an inflow of earthly light is enhanced by an inflow of spiritual light, our thinking is a strange dream and our discourse based on this kind of thinking is fortune-telling.

There is more about levels in *Divine Love and Wisdom* (published in Amsterdam in 1763) §§173–281.

15

Purposes are on the first level, means on the second, and results on the third.

Can anyone fail to see that a purpose is not a means but that it leads to a means, and that a means is not a result but leads to a result? Therefore these are three separate things that follow in sequence.   **17**

In human beings, the purpose is the love in our will, since if we love something, we set it before ourselves and intend it. The faculty of reason in our understanding is the means in us, since our purpose uses our reason to search for means or efficient causes that will make it happen. The result in us is what our body does in response to and accordance with the above. These three exist in us, then, and follow in sequence the way vertical levels do. When all three are present, then the purpose is within the means, and through the means is present in the result, so that in the result the three coexist. This is why the Word says that we will all be judged according to our works, since in them the purpose (the love in our will), the means (the reasoning in our understanding), and the results (our physical actions) are all together. This means that our works reflect our quality as a whole.

[2] If we do not realize this, and fail to draw these distinctions in the objects of thought about which we are reasoning, we cannot avoid limiting the concepts of our thinking to the atoms of Epicurus or the monads of Leibniz or the simple substances of Wolff, and in effect locking our understanding with a dead bolt. This renders us unable to think rationally about spiritual inflow because we cannot conceive of any process by which it would come about, since the author says of his simple substance that if it is divided it disintegrates into nothing. So our understanding remains stuck in its first light, which is derived solely from our physical senses, and does not move a single step beyond it. We cannot help but think that spiritual reality is merely a rarefied form of earthly reality, that animals possess rationality just as we do, and that the soul is like the breath of air that we exhale from our chests when we die—not to mention other notions that shed darkness rather than light.

[3] Since everything in the spiritual world and in the physical world comes about in accord with these levels, as noted in the preceding section, we can see that actual intelligence is recognizing and distinguishing the levels and seeing them in their sequence. Then too, levels allow us to recognize the quality of all people once we know what they love, since, as noted, the purpose they have in their will, the means they have in their understanding, and the deeds of their bodies follow from their love the way a tree develops from its seed and the fruit develops from the tree.

[4] There are three kinds of love: loving heaven, loving the world, and loving ourselves. Loving heaven is spiritual, loving the world is materialistic, and loving ourselves is body-oriented. When our love is spiritual, everything that follows from it, as forms from their essence, receives a spiritual nature. Likewise, if our main love is loving the world or wealth and is therefore materialistic, everything that follows from it, as derivations

from what is primary, receives a materialistic nature. If our main love is loving ourselves, or loving outranking everyone, and is therefore body-oriented, then by the same token everything that follows from it receives a body-oriented nature. This is because when we are possessed by this love, all we focus on is ourselves, so we submerge our minds' thoughts in our bodies.

Consequently, as just noted, if we can identify someone's dominant love and the way it moves from purposes to means and from means to results (the three components that follow in sequence according to vertical levels), then we know the whole person. This is how heaven's angels come to know anyone they are talking with: from the tone of voice they perceive what the person loves, in the face they see an image of that love, and in the gestures they see the shape taken by that love.

16

This shows us the nature of spiritual inflow, from its origin to its results.

Until now, spiritual inflow has been deduced to flow from the soul into the body, but not from God into the soul and from there into the body. This has come about because no one has known anything about the spiritual world and its sun, yet that sun is the source from which all that is spiritual pours forth as from its wellspring; so people have not known anything about the way spiritual realities flow into physical ones. **18**

[2] Since I have been granted the ability to be in the spiritual world and in the physical world at the same time and therefore to see each world and each sun, I am obliged by my conscience to make these things known. What is the use of knowing something except that others should know it as well? The one without the other is like amassing wealth and hiding it away in a chest, simply counting it and admiring it from time to time with no intention of putting it to use. This is nothing but spiritual avarice.

[3] For a full understanding of the reality and nature of spiritual inflow, though, it is necessary to know what *spiritual* is in essence and what *earthly* is, and also what *the human soul* is. For the reception of this brief treatise not to be hobbled by ignorance on these points, it would be beneficial to consult some *accounts of memorable experiences* included

in the book *Marriage Love.* On what *spiritual* is, see the account in §§326–329; on what *the human soul* is, see §315; and on *the inflow of what is spiritual into what is earthly,* see §380, and the fuller treatment in §§415–422.

[Concluding Accounts]

19 To this I will add the following *account of a memorable occurrence.* After the above material was written, I prayed to the Lord to be allowed to talk with some disciples of *Aristotle,* and at the same time with some disciples of *Descartes* and of *Leibniz,* so that I could learn their opinions on the interaction between the soul and the body. After my prayer, nine men were present: three Aristotelians, three Cartesians, and three Leibnizians. They stood around me: the ones who revered Aristotle on my left, the adherents of Descartes on my right, and the supporters of Leibniz behind them. Far off at a distance from us and from each other I saw three men who looked as though they were wearing laurel wreaths, and by an inflowing perception realized that they were the eminent philosophers, the founders themselves. Someone was standing behind Leibniz holding the hem of his garment, and I was told that it was Wolff.

When the nine men noticed each other they started by greeting and addressing each other politely. [2] Before long, though, a spirit came up from the nether regions with a torch in his right hand and waved it in front of their faces. At this the sets of three became hostile and glared at each other, overtaken by an urge to argue and debate.

The Aristotelians (who were also Scholastics) went first. They said, "Can't everyone see that objects flow into the soul through the senses the way people come into a house through its doors, and that the soul has thoughts in response to this inflow? When a young man in love sees his beautiful young bride, is there not a gleam in his eye that carries love for her to his soul? When misers see purses full of coins, surely their senses all catch fire for them, and from their senses they bring this desire into their souls, provoking a craving to take possession of those treasures for themselves. When vain people hear someone paying them compliments, don't their ears prick up and carry the compliments to their souls? Surely the senses serve as entryways that offer our only access to the soul. In the face of this and countless other examples, how can you come to any other conclusion but that inflow comes from the outside world and is physical?"

[3] While listening to this, the adherents of Descartes were holding their fingers to their foreheads; now they removed them and responded to these statements by saying, "Unfortunately, you are talking in terms of the way things seem. Don't you realize that our eyes don't love our young bride on their own? The love comes from our soul. So too, our senses don't crave the coins in the purses on their own; the craving comes from our soul. Our ears seize on the compliments of flatterers in precisely the same way. Surely it is the faculty of perception that enables us to sense. And perception is a function of the soul, not of a physical organ. Tell us this, if you can: What makes the tongue and lips speak except thought? What makes the hands do work except the will? Our thought and our will are functions of our soul, not our body. What causes our eye to see, our ears to hear, and our other organs to feel things except our soul? These and countless other examples will lead anyone whose wisdom rises above what we sense with our bodies to conclude that there is no inflow of the body into the soul but an inflow of the soul into the body, an inflow that we call 'occasional' or 'spiritual' inflow."

[4] When they heard this, the three men who were standing behind the other groups of three, the supporters of Leibniz, spoke up. "We have heard and compared the arguments on each side, and we feel that on many points the second group prevailed, but on many others, the first. So, if you will, let us resolve the dispute." When they were asked how they would do this, they said, "There is no inflow of the soul into the body or of the body into the soul. Instead there is a total and instantaneous coordination of the two at any given moment, a coordination that our celebrated founder has given the lovely name 'preestablished harmony.'"

[5] When they had all finished, the spirit reappeared, this time holding the torch with his left hand, and waved it behind their heads, and all their ideas became confused. They started exclaiming in alarm, "Our souls don't know which way to turn and neither do our bodies, so let's settle the argument by lot. We'll accept whichever lot is drawn first." So they took three slips of paper, wrote *physical inflow* on one, *spiritual inflow* on the second, and *preestablished harmony* on the third, and put them in a hat. They chose someone to do the drawing; the hand went in and pulled out the slip that had "spiritual inflow" written on it. When they looked at it and read it, they all said, "We should accept this because it came out first," but some said this clearly and easily, while others said it vaguely and hesitantly.

[6] Suddenly an angel stood nearby who said, "Don't believe that the slip for spiritual inflow came out by accident. This was providential. Since you were caught up in confused ideas, you were not seeing that it was the truth; but the truth itself presented itself as that slip of paper to the chooser's hand so that you would accept it."

＊　＊　＊　＊　＊　＊

20　I was questioned once as to how I, a scientist, had become a theologian. My answer was, "The same way the Lord made disciples and apostles out of fishermen." I said that I too had been a spiritual fisherman from my youth.

On hearing this, the person asked what a spiritual fisherman was, and I said that in the Word, a fisherman spiritually understood is someone who inquires into and teaches earthly truths and then does the same with spiritual truths, in a rational manner.

[2] When asked what evidence I could provide, I said, "These passages in the Word: 'Then the waters will fail from the sea and the river will be dried up and parched; so the *fishermen* will mourn, and all those who cast a hook into the sea will be sad' (Isaiah 19:5, 8). Again, 'At the river whose waters have been healed, *fishermen* will stand from En-gedi; they will be there to spread their nets. Their *fish* will be of all kinds, like the *fish* of the Great Sea, very many' (Ezekiel 47:9, 10). And again, '"Behold, I will send for many *fishermen,*" says Jehovah, "and they will *fish the children of Israel*"' (Jeremiah 16:16). This shows why the Lord chose fishermen for his disciples and said, 'Come with me, and I will make you *fishers of people*' (Matthew 4:18, 19; Mark 1:16, 17), and why he said to Peter, after he had caught a great many fish, 'From *now on you will catch people*' (Luke 5:9, 10)."

[3] Then from *Revelation Unveiled* I showed why fishermen have this meaning: water means earthly truths (§§50, 932), as does a river (§§409, 932); fish mean people who are devoted to earthly truths (§405), and so fishermen mean people who inquire into such truths and teach them.

[4] When he heard this, my questioner exclaimed, "Now I can understand why the Lord called and chose fishermen to be his disciples, so I am not surprised that he has also chosen you. As you just said, in a spiritual sense you have been a fisherman from your earliest youth—that is, someone who inquired into truths on the earthly level. The reason you

are now inquiring into spiritual truths is that earthly truths serve as their foundation."

He went on to say (since he was a man of reason) that only the Lord would know who was well suited to grasping and presenting the teachings that are part of his new church, whether that would be one of the church leaders or one of their servants. Besides, who among Christian theologians did not first study science in college before they were introduced to theology? How else would they have developed their intelligence?

[5] Finally, he said, "Because you have become a theologian, explain what your theology is." I answered, "Two things are its core principles: *there is one God* and *charity and faith are joined together.*" To this he replied, "Who denies this?" I answered, "The theology of today, if you examine it in depth."

LONDON

1769

Biographical Note

E MANUEL SWEDENBORG (1688–1772) was born Emanuel Swedberg (or Svedberg) in Stockholm, Sweden, on January 29, 1688 (Julian calendar). He was the third of the nine children of Jesper Swedberg (1653–1735) and Sara Behm (1666–1696). At the age of eight he lost his mother. After the death of his only older brother ten days later, he became the oldest living son. In 1697 his father married Sara Bergia (1666–1720), who developed great affection for Emanuel and left him a significant inheritance. His father, a Lutheran clergyman, later became a celebrated and controversial bishop, whose diocese included the Swedish churches in Pennsylvania and in London, England.

After studying at the University of Uppsala (1699–1709), Emanuel journeyed to England, the Netherlands, France, and Germany (1710–1715) to study and work with leading scientists in western Europe. Upon his return he apprenticed as an engineer under the brilliant Swedish inventor Christopher Polhem (1661–1751). He gained favor with Sweden's King Charles XII (1682–1718), who gave him a salaried position as an overseer of Sweden's mining industry (1716–1747). Although Emanuel was engaged, he never married.

After the death of Charles XII, Emanuel was ennobled by Queen Ulrika Eleonora (1688–1741), and his last name was changed to Swedenborg (or Svedenborg). This change in status gave him a seat in the Swedish House of Nobles, where he remained an active participant in the Swedish government throughout his life.

A member of the Royal Swedish Academy of Sciences, he devoted himself to studies that culminated in a number of publications, most notably a comprehensive three-volume work on natural philosophy and metallurgy (1734) that brought him recognition across Europe as a scientist. After 1734 he redirected his research and publishing to a study of anatomy in search of the interface between the soul and body, making several significant discoveries in physiology.

From 1743 to 1745 he entered a transitional phase that resulted in a shift of his main focus from science to theology. Throughout the rest of his life he maintained that this shift was brought about by Jesus Christ, who appeared to him, called him to a new mission, and opened his perception to a permanent dual consciousness of this life and the life after death.

He devoted the last decades of his life to studying Scripture and publishing eighteen theological titles that draw on the Bible, reasoning, and his own spiritual experiences. These works present a Christian theology with unique perspectives on the nature of God, the spiritual world, the Bible, the human mind, and the path to salvation.

Swedenborg died in London on March 29, 1772 (Gregorian calendar), at the age of eighty-four.